OLYMPIAN
BRISTOL • LEYLAND • VOLVO

MARTIN S. CURTIS

Ian Allan
PUBLISHING

Contents

Front cover: **Badgerline all-Leyland Olympian 9004 (G904 TWS) as introduced to service in Bath during October 1989.**
M. S. Curtis

Back cover (upper): **Kowloon Motor Bus was the Olympian's most important customer, taking more into stock than any other operator. Seen here is 3BL117 (DH 7958), an Alexander-bodied 12m example.**
M. S. Curtis

Back cover (lower): **In immaculate condition, 721 (A721 YFS) was among Lothian's second batch of ECW-bodied, Bristol-built Olympians which included a revised interior layout and coolant header tanks on the offside.**
Author's collection

Previous page: **Three ECW-bodied Olympians from the Northern General fleet (from left to right Nos 3583, 3654 and 3740) wearing Tyne & Wear PTE-style yellow and white livery.**
Photobus

First published 2010

ISBN 978 0 7110 3479 2

Published by Ian Allan Publishing

an imprint of Ian Allan Publishing Ltd, Hersham, Surrey, KT12 4RG
Printed in England by Ian Allan Printing Ltd, Hersham, Surrey, KT12 4RG

Code: 1008/B2

Distributed in the United States of America and Canada by BookMasters Distribution Services

Visit the Ian Allan Publishing website at www.ianallanpublishing.com

Foreword

The Olympian was without doubt an extremely successful design which was produced in vast numbers over a 20-year period. It was however to suffer from an unprecedented level of both political interference and industrial uncertainty as production was moved from factory to factory.

Conceived by teams of designers at Brislington, in Bristol, and Leyland, Lancashire, the model came to represent a number of significant 'lasts'. It was the last bus chassis design to be built by Bristol Commercial Vehicles, the last double-decker bodied by Charles H. Roe of Leeds, the last design produced by Eastern Coach Works of Lowestoft, the last product from the Leyland National plant at Workington and the last bus to bear the once mighty 'Leyland' name. Despite this it was adopted by Volvo, which continued production in Scotland and whose influence not only brought the model new success in home markets but also ensured that it continued to represent one of the UK's major motor-vehicle exports.

Throughout the most turbulent times for bus manufacturing the Olympian remained in demand, and, despite all the difficulties and disruption placed in its path, the model itself not only survived but was market leader — truly an indication of the success of its design. Sadly, however, with the loss of so many historic and experienced British bus manufacturers during the period of Olympian production, it is difficult to imagine how its success could ever be repeated.

Martin S. Curtis, FCILT, M Inst TA
Saltford, Bristol
July 2010

The sight of bus chassis being driven around the roads of Bristol and North Somerset had become familiar over decades. Here an Olympian chassis returns from a test run to Chatsworth Road, Brislington, the approach to the BCV works. The practice of driving bare chassis on test or for delivery to the coachworks ceased with the closure of Bristol.
M. S. Curtis

Acknowledgements

Four Volvo Olympians with Alexander coachwork from the Citybus fleet (from left to right Nos 990, 1028, 944 and 1004) at Shau Kei Wan on Hong Kong Island.
M. S. Curtis

The preparation of a book such as this can only succeed with the generous support, encouragement and welcome contributions of all kinds from others. In the case of this account of the Olympian, photographs are individually credited, while many friends and colleagues assisted in tracking down information and photographic material. This has been given willingly, although it is a reflection of the strength of feeling associated with the plant closures of over a quarter of a century ago that many still passionately believe at least some of those factories should have remained in business, allowing production of high-quality passenger vehicles to continue. I am particularly indebted to Ron Cave and Don Ottrey from Bristol Commercial Vehicles, Stuart Bond, Stewart J. Brown and David Burnicle, formerly of Leyland, and Jim Anderson of Volvo, all of whom have over a considerable period provided valuable information. Allan Macfarlane and Mike Walker kindly read through drafts, while further assistance was given by Gavin Booth, Collin Brougham-Field, Maurice Doggett, Stephen Cho, Allan Field, Brian Jackson, Allen Janes, Brian Longley, David McConn, Scott Mitchell, Kate Moon, Phil Sposito, Stephen Morris, Mike Sutcliffe and Derek White.

The PSV Circle, Bristol Industrial Museum, the BBC Motion Gallery and the Classic Irish Buses website are also gratefully acknowledged for making available material used in research.

Before the Olympian

The period following World War 2 represented the boom years for the British bus industry, passenger loadings reaching their peak during the 1950s, which period also witnessed the gradual replacement of tram and trolleybus services (where provided) by motor buses.

The operating industry was largely locally structured, each town or area having at least one operator, the largest of which was London Transport, with its huge fleet of red (Central) buses encircled by green (Country) buses. Elsewhere many towns and cities enjoyed municipally owned transport, while most of the remainder of Britain was served by large regional bus companies which formed part of the British Electric Traction, Tilling or Scottish groups. A large number of independent operators of varying size provided the remaining local (stage-carriage) services.

The standard British double-decker continued to be front-engined with a rear entrance and platform (which was sometimes enclosed by doors) and was crew-operated. Manufacturers of the period included AEC, Bristol, Daimler, Dennis, Guy and Leyland, all of which remained independent of each other.

In 1948, as part of the then Labour Government's commitment to nationalise much of the country's transport industry, the Scottish and Tilling groups came under state control. Whilst most of these group companies were bus operators, included among the latter was the Bristol bus-manufacturing works, together with Eastern Coach Works of Lowestoft.

Unfortunately, under the terms of their state ownership, both Bristol and ECW were immediately restricted to selling their products to operators under state control. However, this did not prevent innovation, and the two companies collaborated closely in developing and producing the Lodekka, a low-height, low-entrance double-decker which set standards for other manufacturers to follow. Prior to its introduction in 1949 two distinct double-deck bus designs had evolved, known as 'highbridge' and 'lowbridge', the latter having reduced headroom and an inconvenient side-gangway arrangement on the upper deck in order to reduce overall height. Standard highbridge double-deckers were approximately 14ft 6in high, but the lowbridge configuration, which reduced this by some 12 inches, was used on many routes with high demand that passed under obstructions such as railway bridges.

In general, town and city services used highbridge buses, while the lowbridge design was commonly to be found on country or longer-distance services, although there were many exceptions to this pattern of allocation. The Lodekka cleverly offered central gangways on both decks within the overall height of a lowbridge bus, this being achieved by offsetting the driveline, which connected to a new design of dropped-centre rear axle. Later examples featured a forward entrance, which was gradually gaining acceptance on double-deckers of all makes, and the Lodekka remained in production until 1968. Dennis also built the model under licence as the Loline, in order to make it available to operators outside the state sector.

The Lodekka was followed by a completely different approach to double-deck bus design from Leyland, which developed a rear-engined arrangement with power unit positioned transversely, while the entrance was located alongside the driver, ahead of a set-back front axle.

This model was named Atlantean, and from the time of its appearance in 1956

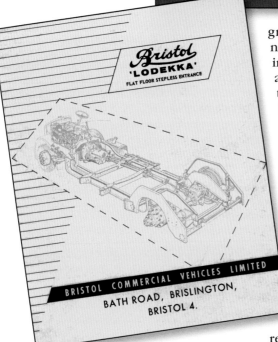

gradually — over the next decade or so — influenced a change by all manufacturers to this configuration, not least because this layout permitted double-deckers to be one-man-operated without a conductor, which became permissible from 1966.

Initially the Atlantean could not be offered in low-height form other than by adopting a side gangway at the rear of the upper deck in lowbridge style, but from 1960 an outwardly similar rear-engined model from Daimler combined the rear-engine layout with a dropped-centre rear axle, offering the 'best for both worlds', as claimed in contemporary advertising. The Daimler model was christened Fleetline.

Henceforth the Atlantean and Fleetline competed for business, and this was to continue after Leyland had gained control of Daimler in 1968. Indeed, following trials with both models, it was the Fleetline that won large, prestigious orders from London Transport in the 1970s, only for the type to be withdrawn prematurely when LT decided it was not, after all, suited to the capital's operating conditions. This resulted in large numbers' reappearing throughout the provinces with operators eager to snap them up in order to modernise their fleets and accelerate conversions to one-man operation.

In later years, following transfer of Fleetline production from Coventry to Lancashire in 1973, the Fleetline was badged as a Leyland model.

By this time Leyland had also gained control of AEC (together with the Park Royal and Roe bodybuilding concerns) and Guy Motors, but the situation at Bristol Commercial Vehicles was rather different. In order to release Bristol and ECW from sales restrictions, an exchange of shares occurred during 1965 between its parent organisation, the Transport Holding Company, and the Leyland Motor Corporation. This gave Leyland a 25% stake in Bristol and ECW, while the THC took almost 29% of Park Royal Vehicles.

Bristol (and ECW) began a close association with Leyland from this point, but, much to the surprise and embarrassment of Leyland management,

Above: **After trials with both Atlanteans and Fleetlines, London Transport opted for large numbers of Fleetlines with dual-door bodywork, forming its DM/DMS class which grew to be over 2,600 strong before premature withdrawal commenced. Bodywork was provided by Metro-Cammell or, as in the case of DM1018 (GHV 18N) seen here, Park Royal.**
M. S. Curtis

Left: **The Atlantean evolved into the AN68 version. Here two Roe-bodied examples from 1979, AN204/14 (EPH 204/14V), pass at Gravesend while operating London Country's route 480, the Atlantean's characteristic engine 'bustle' being clearly visible on AN204. The windscreen design was carried over to Roe's Olympian bodywork.**
Author's collection

Bristol's single-deck RE model proceeded to win significant orders — including from previously loyal Leyland customers. In 1966, meanwhile, Bristol announced its new VR double-decker, with engine mounted longitudinally at the rear, but from 1968 this was offered in revised form as the VRT, with the engine mounted transversely, Atlantean-style.

Arguably the most important development of 1968 was the passing of a new Transport Act, which was to have a significant influence on both the operating and manufacturing sides of the British bus industry. Amongst other things it created the first four Passenger Transport Authorities (and Executives to undertake the operations) in the conurbations of Tyneside, Merseyside, the West Midlands and Greater Manchester (where operations were known initially by the acronym SELNEC — South East Lancashire, North East Cheshire). Another provision of the Act was the creation of the National Bus Company (a move prompted by the state-owned Transport Holding Co's takeover of BET's British bus operations), which took control of services in England and Wales with effect from 1 January 1969. The following year saw further changes to the operating industry, as from 1 January 1970, under the terms of the Transport (London) Act 1969, London Transport's Country Area became the responsibility of a new NBC subsidiary, London Country Bus Services Ltd.

An early decision within NBC resulted in a reduction of the state's interests in Bristol and ECW from 75% to 50%, the British Leyland Motor Corporation (as it had become) eagerly increasing its interest to control the remaining half-shares of the companies. However, whilst the manufacture of Britain's buses remained almost exclusively the preserve of British companies, 1970 saw the seemingly innocuous trial by London Transport of a Metro-Scania single-decker, which featured the Swedish manufacturer's running units within a British-built Metro-Cammell body. In later years it would be followed by a double-deck version, the Metropolitan, which in turn led directly to the development of the Metrobus double-decker, produced from 1978. The Metrobus featured a much higher British content,

but both Scania and its Swedish riva Volvo were by then independently makin significant inroads into the UK commercial-vehicle market.

The late 1960s saw a substantial move awa from double-deck buses in favour of singl deckers, which more conveniently allowe operators to convert services from two-ma crews to one-man operation. A 36ft-lon single-decker was capable of almos matching the seating capacity of a 1950 double-decker, which in many cases replaced. From 1968 the Government offere a New Bus Grant to operators purchasin buses suitable for one-man operatio accelerating the conversion process.

With operators increasingly favourin single-deckers, by far the most successfu rear-engined design of the period wa Bristol's RE, which was available in variou lengths. Recognising the trend, Leylan embarked on a project to produce a nev highly standardised single-deck design, anc with substantial Government funding, new purpose-built factory was constructe at Lilyhall in Workington, Cumberland — a area of high unemployment. Here the nev model entered production from 1972, buil by a workforce from largely outside th motor industry, employing a process simila to that used for the mass production of cars

Like Bristol and ECW the compan producing this new model was a join Leyland/NBC enterprise named Leylanc National Ltd, and the model itself woulc reflect this situation, being known as th Leyland National.

Assembled entirely at the Workingtor site, the Leyland National was a highl standardised model which (in contrast tc other designs) allowed operators littl scope in terms of influencing the body layout or finish. Based on a strong bu heavy integral structure, it included controversially, Leyland's 500-series fixed head, turbocharged engine, mountec horizontally at the rear. Moreover, althoug proclaimed as a means of persuading th public to return to bus travel, the Leylanc National often had the opposite effect, earl examples having spartan, almost auster interiors. It also featured a unique saloon heating system, equipment for which wa contained in a roof-mounted pod, hot ai being forced downwards from cantrai level. Fuel economy was poor, but the rgonomically designed cab was good, although many of the controls and other ittings proved less than robust.

Reflecting anticipated demand, the new plant had capacity to build up to 2,000 vehicles per year, but although NBC operators and other British customers were ultimately prevented from ordering the Bristol RE, production of the Leyland National never reached the levels envisaged. Indeed, by the mid-1970s the operating industry had also changed direction, once again opting for more double-deckers, which were increasingly being worked without a conductor.

Despite its close relationship with NBC, Leyland was somewhat dismayed that this single-deck design, which it believed the operating industry wanted, had failed to attract anticipated levels of business. This was in spite of attempts to increase its appeal with, in later years, different engine, seating and livery options. Even the Leyland National 2, which reintroduced a front-mounted radiator (in Bristol style) and a naturally aspirated engine, was unable to turn the situation around, and eventually — almost in desperation — the Workington body design was adopted as the basis of a railbus.

Inevitably Leyland turned its attention to double-deck development once more and in 1973 unveiled its design for what at first appeared to be a double-deck Leyland National. This was Project B15, which revived the model name 'Titan' when

While Leyland was developing the B15 Bristol Commercial Vehicles updated its VRT double-decker to Series 3 form, with an encapsulated engine compartment and air ducts leading to cooling vents above the waistband — features that were later incorporated into the Olympian. Prior to registration, this pre-production Series 3 (destined to become Hants & Dorset 3321) is viewed on test near the Bristol works during July 1975. *M. S. Curtis*

Above: **The vast majority of Bristol VRs received ECW coachwork, and in the deregulated environment many lasted on front-line services for 30 years. As the standard double-decker for the National Bus Company the type could be found throughout England and Wales, although dual-door versions were less common. Here Bristol Omnibus 5048 (LEU 256P) climbs Sandy Park Road, Brislington, during the winter of 1978/9.**
M. S. Curtis

Right: **B15 prototype 04 (NHG 732P), with test equipment aboard, photographed wearing red livery in Buckingham Palace Road, Victoria, during early London trials. The date was 8 March 1976.**
M. S. Curtis

Left: **B15-04** spent two periods working on London Transport's route 24 and is here quietly entering Chalk Farm garage, where it was based. The asymmetric rear-window arrangement and odd styling above the engine compartment, housing the radiator on the offside, was in contrast to the remainder of the body, which was well proportioned.
M. S. Curtis

Below: **B15-02 (FHG 592S)** also served as a demonstrator and coincidentally is seen here also working on a service 24. This time, however, the location is Cardiff, where it was operating during June 1979 in the hope of attracting more orders. Livery was yellow and grey.
M. S. Curtis

production commenced in 1978. Leyland failed to interest either NBC or any other operator in directly sharing responsibility for production, but this model was aimed squarely at the large urban Passenger Transport Authority fleets and, most significantly, London Transport. Following plans to build this model at the AEC factory at Southall (considered by many to be the traditional home of London bus building) it was in fact initially produced by Park Royal Vehicles with mechanical units from Leyland. Built to a highbridge layout, 4.4m (14ft 5in) tall and 9.6m (31ft 5in) long, it featured integral construction with a sophisticated specification which included a Hydracyclic fully automatic gearbox, power hydraulic brakes and self-levelling air suspension. With the radiator above the engine compartment, power was at first provided by Leyland's vertical turbocharged Leyland 500 series (suspended rather than supported from below), but Gardner and Leyland TL11 engines were soon offered as alternatives. Handling was extremely good, and the excellent cab layout was carried over from the Leyland National.

Unfortunately the Titan also shared the National's inflexibility, for although the body design was of more traditional construction and finish than the single-decker it too offered operators little opportunity to request variations from the overall standard design.

London Transport opted to purchase the Titan as one of two standard double-deck models for its fleet, the other being the MCW Metrobus, and in the late 1970s and early '80s both entered London service in their hundreds. Elsewhere, however, the Titan failed to win substantial orders, and despite limited interest from a few other local-authority fleets, including PTEs, it was for London that the vast majority would be built.

Meanwhile, developments occurred between NBC and Leyland in terms of their association as joint owners of manufacturing companies. Prior to 1969 the benefit of having Bristol and ECW as in-house bus builders for the state-owned fleets was considered a major asset, the close collaboration between these manufacturers and the operators being akin to a family relationship. Had this continued

following the creation of NBC, vehicle finished to truly impressive standards migh have resulted, but instead Leyland sough increasingly to influence productio including the day-to-day running of th works. Indeed, NBC often treated Leylan more as an adversary rather than partner i bus design and construction, appearin content for its engineers to becom embroiled in relatively minor matters whil Leyland held sway over fundamental desig issues.

Nevertheless, a new organisation ha been created during the 1970s to overse bus production from the various factorie and plants in which both Leyland and NB had an interest. This was Bus Manufacturer Ltd, a holding company for Bristo Commercial Vehicles, Eastern Coach Work and the Leyland National plant a Workington. By the end of the decad following a further transfer of shares, Par Royal Vehicles Ltd, together with Charles F Roe, the Leeds-based coachbuilder, had als been acquired by Bus Manufacturer (Holdings) Ltd.

All these developments would influenc future production, especially as by 1980 th Leyland Titan was appearing in significan numbers in London but failing to attrac many orders from other operators, despit its extensive development programme.

The Titan was undoubtedly a wel designed vehicle, but its sophistication an inflexible design caused most operators t continue ordering Leyland Atlanteans Fleetlines or Bristol VRTs to meet thei double-deck requirements, while severa other manufacturers were also carefull considering the British market for double deck buses, including Dennis, Foden, Scani and Volvo Ailsa. To some extent this wa being encouraged by operators (which wer concerned by Leyland's near-monopolisti position) and coachbuilders (which coul see business slipping away if Leylan increased its share of the market with a integral double-decker, as it had with th Leyland National saloon).

The Titan was built to highbridge layou which was entirely suitable for most urba operating conditions. However, th National Bus and Scottish group companie required double-deckers which wer predominantly of low-height design with significantly reduced overall height in orde

West Midlands 7001
(WDA IT) was an early
production Titan, the first of a
batch of five Park Royal-
bodied examples purchased
for evaluation by this
operator. It was among
vehicles provided for the park-
and-ride shuttle to and from
the National Exhibition
Centre, Birmingham, during
the 1978 Motor Show.
M. S. Curtis

o pass safely under low bridges, trees, and other obstructions which featured throughout their operating territories. The Titan was available only in one basic length, and some operators were looking to increase this to meet their particular circumstances. Moreover, the limited choice of body design not only displeased UK operators, but also many overseas who would not countenance the purchase of buses which failed to offer the opportunity for bodywork to be added locally — providing support for their own economy and employment. In its efforts to secure business by offering the Titan as a standardised, integrated design, Leyland was therefore in danger of jeopardising its own export trade which had been successfully established over several decades, both in former colonial and entirely new markets.

There is little doubt that Leyland was seeking to rationalise its double-deck range with Titan being the first choice (as Leyland National had become for single-deckers) allowing the gradual phasing out of Atlanteans, Fleetlines and Bristol's VRT. However, Leyland had not, in fact, lost sight of the need for more flexibility and as early as February 1977 the trade press reported that consideration was being given to producing a chassis incorporating B15 components, which would meet low-height and export requirements. This was the first indication of a design that would eventually become the Olympian.

Above: **The bleak appearance of a newly delivered Leyland National 2 saloon, destined to become Bristol Omnibus 3522, awaiting preparation for service during the summer of 1980. Although improved compared with earlier Leyland Nationals — but in stark contrast to the products of other bodybuilders — these vehicles continued to be supplied with austere single-colour paintwork, leaving the operator to provide relief, fleetnames and other finishing touches before entry into service. Note, however, that by this time a clear family resemblance was emerging between National, Titan and B45.**
M. S. Curtis

Right: **A Workington-built Leyland Titan, which when completed in 1984 became London Transport T1030 (A630 THV). Seating was provided for 70, while Gardner supplied the power.**
M. S. Curtis

The B45s

In June 1977, when Leyland officially launched its B15 as the Titan, it was confirmed that a chassis-based version of Titan would be offered to meet low-height requirements and would be made available to any bodybuilder, allowing the Atlantean, Fleetline and Bristol VR to be discontinued. There was even speculation that the Titan chassis might be produced by Bristol Commercial Vehicles, much of the body requirements being met by Bristol's traditional partner — Eastern Coach Works.

Significantly, Bristol had from the mid-1970s been building a new single-deck chassis, limited production of which continued into the 1980s. This was the Leyland B21 (occasionally also known as the Lion), which consisted of Leyland National running units fitted into a traditional chassis frame (with the characteristically Bristol front-mounted radiator) which could then be exported for local bodying — in exactly the way it was planned to produce Titan-derived chassis to meet export orders.

Having witnessed growing interest in the MCW Metrobus, a new Dennis Dominator chassis to rival the Fleetline, and even collaboration between Foden and Northern Counties to produce a rear-engined double-deck model, Leyland decided to draw on the experience of BCV's staff to develop a new rear-engined bus chassis, with support from Leyland's own personnel, who shared responsibility for the design.

At this stage a proposed model name for this new chassis was 'Unicorn', this mythical creature having long been associated with the City & County of Bristol, being incorporated prominently within its coat of arms. Although not ultimately adopted, for a while this appears to have been the accepted model name at Brislington; indeed, BCV had previously issued lapel badges and key-fobs which combined the image of a unicorn with the Bristol name. Upon receiving a directive that the Leyland name was to be applied to the new chassis BCV somewhat optimistically created a full (and rather dated) badge design incorporating a unicorn taken directly from the Bristol coat-of-arms. Leyland, of course, had other ideas, and one can imagine a degree of tension between the works' respective teams over this emotive issue!

By the summer of 1979 considerable development work had progressed with the Titan-derived chassis, which by then had been given project code B45. The first chassis had indeed been built by Bristol Commercial Vehicles and subsequently sent to Lowestoft, where, by September, a body shell had been completed by ECW.

Meanwhile, elsewhere in the Leyland bus-building empire, considerable difficulties were arising. AEC's Southall works had closed during the summer of 1979, and production problems for the Titan at Park Royal, where management and staff had failed to agree terms, had resulted in an announcement that it too was to close. Within months two of London's principal bus-building factories would be no more, and a new home was being urgently sought for the Titan, which now found itself

Co-operation between Bristol and Leyland engineers was probably never closer than during the design stage of the B45. The chassis required a new front-axle and suspension arrangement to be mounted within the perimeter frame, a trial version of which was constructed by Bristol's experimental department. This was then fitted to an old Leyland Worldmaster chassis (fitted with a 1950s lorry cab) which formed test rig MTR42 and was driven extensively around the Leyland test track in Lancashire to ensure the design was sound.
Leyland Vehicles Ltd

in trouble; very rapidly both West Midlands PTE and London Transport announced that they were switching large orders to MCW's Metrobus while uncertainty over Titan production remained.

Suddenly the B45 was thrust into far greater prominence, because if the Titan failed to continue, not only might the B45 have to be substituted to meet demand; it would also be required to carry forward all of Titan's development costs.

Preparations for a shift in favour of B45s were underway, with chassis production at Bristol and bodywork built largely at Lowestoft. If demand for bodywork could not be met by ECW (as Leyland's other rear-engined double-deck models were phased out), capacity at Charles H. Roe of Leeds would also be needed.

Traditionally, staff relations at both Bristol and ECW were extremely good, with few industrial-relations problems, each having a well-motivated workforce producing high quality chassis and bodywork respectively. This gave Leyland confidence to announce at the end of 1979 that Titan production would continue at Lowestoft, with bodywork constructed on underframes

B45-01 as seen in public for the first time on 21 May 1980, when this frame formed one of a sequence of flash cuts (which revealed both this bus and B45-02) broadcast by the BBC in an edition of its series *The Risk Business*, entitled 'The Clash of the Titans'. Prominent 'LEYLAND' lettering had been fitted prior to filming.
BBC Motion Gallery

assembled at the Leyland National plant. Unfortunately, Leyland had failed to recognise that ECW comprised a highly skilled workforce with, in many cases, trades handed down through several generations. Titan assembly would involve an influx of unskilled staff, and the ECW workforce was having none of it.

With a second B45 completed, 1980 commenced optimistically for the Passenger Vehicle Division of Leyland Vehicles Ltd, but by early February the decision not to accept Titan production at Lowestoft had become known, and Leyland had to search elsewhere for a new home for Titan — amid veiled threats over the long-term future of ECW. The Titan was to survive, however, and during April it was announced that production would recommence at the Leyland National plant at Workington, where there was ample capacity and no conflict over the skills issue.

A month later, on 21 May 1980, Leyland pulled a stunt which would help revive its fortunes. During the evening the BBC broadcast an edition in its television series *The Risk Business*, which on this occasion examined the state of Britain's bus-building industry. This was the period immediately before the general availability of domestic video recorders, and whilst of interest to the public at large, people from the whole of the bus industry would be tuned in. The programme considered the merits of London's Titans and Metrobuses relative to its Routemasters, as well as the reliability of other models; it also examined new entrants from overseas manufacturers. Also included were footage and interviews recorded at Leyland's test track, where, in the final minutes, the B45 was revealed — the first time it had been seen in public. It was a masterstroke.

Although the programme was edited to show shots in quick succession, it was possible to identify the first two B45 prototypes, which combined Titan styling with that of ECW bodywork for the Bristol VRT. The upper deck closely followed the Titan design, with similar front, rear and side windows and roof domes. Side windows of similar size were employed for the lower-deck glazing, which was shallower than used for Titan as a result of the low overall height of 13ft 8in (4.2m). At the rear the engine compartment was

B45-01, as finished by ECW but lacking interior trim, panelling and fittings. Its curved BET windscreen and VRT front dash was combined with the angular styling already seen on the B15 Titan. It would be extensively tested before full production commenced. *ECW*

neatly enclosed with an upward-folding access door, while the area above was incorporated into the body shape in similar style to ECW's bodywork for the Bristol VRT, albeit slightly more angular, to match the Titan's appearance. Ventilation for the engine compartment followed the method used for Series 3 VRTs, with ducting connecting grilles above waist level on the side and rear corners.

B45-01 supported a dual-door body shell without interior trim or fittings and spent much time undergoing extensive testing on Leyland's test track. Its frontal appearance differed from the Titan in that it carried over from the VRT a BET-style curved windscreen, while its dash panel and grille were also of Bristol VRT design. It was painted all-over red, with B45-01 numbering on its side panels, and allocated the number EX14 in ECW's experimental series.

B45-02 was finished to full service standards and carried NBC red livery with a white relief band and Ribble fleetnames, being destined to enter service with that operator as No 2100. With body EX15, it appeared unregistered in the TV programme. It too featured a BET-style windscreen together with a completely new design of front dash panel with a full-width black strip which incorporated the front lights and grille and had a strong family resemblance to both the Titan and the Leyland National 2.

Despite being Bristol-built, both vehicles carried prominent white 'LEYLAND' block lettering across their grilles and Leyland roundels on their hub centres, confirming Leyland's desire to suppress all except its own name. Shortly after Leyland had taken a stake in Bristol Commercial Vehicles a handful of Bristol REs for operation in Lancashire, together with a batch of Bristol VRLs exported to South Africa, had carried Leyland badges. Now, with Leyland influence over day-to-day affairs at the works constantly increasing, Bristol was producing the B21 as a Leyland model rather than under its own name. As NBC continued to own 50% of Bristol, one might have expected that it would have sought to retain the Bristol name — or at the very least, used the Leyland National title to reflect joint ownership. That this was not to be was perhaps indicative of NBC's approach towards bus manufacturing. It now appeared that the B45 model was also to be badged as a Leyland, although this was not to be quite as clear-cut as initially seemed to be the case.

The first printed picture of a B45 appeared a month after the BBC

Above: **B45-01 was eventually sold, in July 1983, to Stevensons of Uttoxeter, where it was brought up to full service standards. It is parked here at Stevensons' Spath depot, having been converted to single-door layout but still awaiting entry into service, during September 1984.**
M. S. Curtis

Right: **Having received fleet number 99 and registration Q246 FVT (the 'Q' prefix indicating a vehicle of indeterminate age), B45-01 is seen in a later version of Stevensons livery while operating a local service at Rugeley during December 1989.**
M. S. Curtis

Far left: **A rear view of B45-02, recorded outside Eastern Coach Works upon completion. Allocated body number EX15, this was the first B45 finished to full service standards, although manufacturers' badges had still to be added. The engine compartment featured a fold-up rear section and hinged side panels, allowing excellent access to the power unit. The ventilation grilles above the waistline followed VRT3 practice, while the staircase occupied a longer area than would be the case on production models.** *ECW*

Above left: **The press launch for B45-02 was held at Preston bus station, where the bus is seen posed for photographs. Prominent 'LEYLAND' lettering has been added to the grille, although the registration plate has been removed. On subsequent models the white waistband would continue over the windscreen, and the wheels (here painted in standard NBC grey) would be black.** *Ian Allan Library*

programme was broadcast, NBC's staff newspaper *Bus News* for June 1980 including a view of B45-02 at Preston bus station, discreetly tucked away at the bottom of an inside page! A few weeks later, a more prominent version of this picture followed in the trade press, from which it was possible to discern the registration carried as UHV 995V. However, upon entering service with Ribble Motor Services at Blackpool during August 1980 (when it became clear that this bus was powered by a Gardner engine) it displayed a different registration number — DBV 100W.

Above left: **The first of many Olympian publicity brochures included no fewer than nine photographs of B45-02, together with chassis pictures and technical information.**

Left: **A nearside view of B45-02 at Preston, this time displaying dummy registration UHV 995V. The divided bench seat over the front wheel arch was another feature not perpetuated on production bodies.** *Author's collection*

Right: **Upon entering service as Ribble 2100 prototype B45-02 carried registration DBV 100W. Seen participating in a Bus Driver of the Year Competition, it also displays an additional fleetname, above the front grille, and an early-style Olympian badge. Of greater significance, however, are the wheels, now painted black to indicate to NBC engineers that they are spigot-mounted.**
Author's collection

Right: **In due course Ribble became part of Stagecoach, and in 1997 B45-02 was transferred to the group's neighbouring Cumberland subsidiary. It is seen near Shap during June 2000, looking remarkably well turned out for a 20-year-old bus.**
Tom Curtis

Right: **A rear view of B45-02 with Cumberland (in which fleet it retained its original number), showing the original design of rear panelling and engine cover.**
Tom Curtis

Speculation about a model name for the B45 was growing as the Motor Show, to be held in October at the National Exhibition Centre (NEC) in Birmingham, approached. By September, however, it had become an 'open secret', and at the beginning of October, in advance of the Show, Leyland officially launched the B45 as the Olympian. The name seemed to fit extremely well as successor to Leyland's original rear-engined double-decker, the Atlantean. It was, however, a name that Leyland had employed previously, for a small quantity of integral single-deckers produced during the 1950s.

At the launch it was finally possible to obtain full details of the new chassis, which clearly embodied both Bristol and Leyland thinking and incorporated many Titan components. Power was provided by Gardner 6LXB (177bhp) or Leyland TL11 (170bhp) units, the engine being suspended as seen previously on the B15, which arrangement avoided the structural problems suffered by models with engines supported from below. Leyland's Hydracyclic gearbox with integral retarder was included, as were full air brakes.

Air suspension was provided all round, and whilst the front beam axle was new the rear axle was of dropped-centre design, which, although employed in the Titan, had first been introduced by Bristol more than three decades earlier. The chassis included

perimeter framing, something developed by Bristol for its semi-integral Lodekka and later VRL models, while another Bristol feature was the radiator, which was mounted at the front to take advantage of the natural air flow as the bus was in motion. Even the shallow fuel tanks were taken straight from the Bristol VRT, while the ergonomically designed cab was the latest version shared with the Titan and the National 2. The frame itself was of Bristol design and was composed of channel sections bolted together using 'sticky bolts', which were impregnated with an adhesive for added security.

The chassis was available with either 16ft 3in (4.9m) or 18ft 6in (5.6m) wheelbase, offering overall lengths of 31ft 5in (9.6m) or 33ft 8in (10.3m) respectively, while further flexibility enabled operators to specify full- or low-height bodywork.

When the Motor Show opened on 17 October the Olympian stole the show, no fewer than five pre-production examples (compared with just one Titan — the last to be built at Park Royal) being on display, between them demonstrating how versatile the model could be. On Leyland Vehicles' own stand was B45-04, an ECW-bodied 77-seat low-height bus (with body EX16) which followed closely the pattern of the second prototype, weighing a commendable 9,800kg but in this case wearing the livery of Scottish Bus Group

Above left: **The 1980 Motor Show saw no fewer than five B45s on display. ECW body EX16 was carried by B45-04, exhibited in the colours of Alexander (Midland), with 'Midland Scottish' fleetnames. With more compact staircase and other detail modifications, it set the standard for the production ECW low-height bodies which followed. Registered OMS 910W and given fleet number MRO1 by Midland, this bus was transferred to Alexander (Northern) a year later, following trials with various Scottish Bus Group companies.** *Paul Dudley*

Above: **This rear view of MRO1 shows that the rear numberplate position has reverted to the waistband, as on ECW-bodied VRTs. Just visible alongside on Leyland's show stand is the front wheel and frame of B45-06, a left-hand-drive vehicle exhibited in chassis form.** *Paul Dudley*

Right: Two Olympians appeared on the Alexander stand at the 1980 Show, with different versions of that builder's new R-type body design. B45-03, with seating for 76, was destined for Greater Glasgow PTE and was powered by a Leyland TL11 unit. It became LO1, with registration VGB 364W. Note the 'Strathclyde' fleetname. *M. S. Curtis*

Far right: The second Alexander-bodied Olympian was B45-07, a long-wheelbase version with dual-door bodywork featuring 3+2 seating to achieve a capacity of 97. It boldly displayed the destination 'SINGAPORE' — where it operated initially, with registration SBS 5396B. *M. S. Curtis*

Right: The seating capacity of B45-07 was reduced to 84 before it commenced trials in Singapore, after which it returned to the UK. In 1987 it was sold to City of Oxford Motor Services as 999, receiving new British registration PWL 999W. After replacement of its sliding tropical windows it also received an ECW-style lower-deck windscreen, dash and grille. Used almost exclusively on Park & Ride services, it is seen in St Aldates, Oxford, during April 1992. *M. S. Curtis*

subsidiary Alexander (Midland), to which fleet it was allocated MRO1 (OMS 910W). Alongside was long-wheelbase left-hand-drive chassis B45-06, destined for Baghdad.

Two further examples could be found on the stand of Walter Alexander & Co (Coachbuilders) Ltd, of Falkirk, supporting this firm's new R-type body design. B45-03 was a Leyland TL11-engined, standard-wheelbase example for Greater Glasgow PTE (with fleet number LO1 and displaying the operator's new 'Strathclyde' fleetname in advance of its formal renaming), while the second bus on this stand was B45-07, a long-wheelbase 97-seater to dual-door layout, also with Leyland power unit, which

was to be an Asian demonstrator and accordingly displayed the destination 'Singapore'.

The final Olympian on display (B45-05) could be found on the stand of Northern Counties Motor & Engineering Co, the highly respected bodybuilder based in Wigan. This was a standard-wheelbase, Leyland-engined bus finished in the colours of Greater Manchester PTE (the successor to SELNEC) as its 1451 (NJA 568W). With a single entrance/exit, this vehicle offered seating for 73 passengers and was built to an intermediate height of 14ft 2in (4.3m).

Two further pre-production B45s were also produced before full production

Left: **After being displayed in chassis form at the 1980 Show TL11-powered B45-06 received this 86-seat ECW body — which incorporated peaked domes, full-depth sliding windows and a much-simplified grille and front panelling — for demonstration in Baghdad, where Leyland Atlanteans were already in service. It remained in Iraq for several years before returning to the UK but failed to attract further orders.** *ECW*

Left: **The Baghdad demonstrator was sold to Calypso Bus Service, Gibraltar, in 1990, but was not registered (as G 77960) until five years later. The company was later restructured to become Calypso Transport Ltd. Curiously this operator uses Baghdad livery for its fleet (which also includes a Baghdad-style Atlantean). Looking in astonishingly good condition in view of its age and history, B45-06 was photographed in Gibraltar in January 2006.** *M. S. Curtis*

commenced. These received chassis numbers B45-08 and -09 and represented part of an order for three ECW-bodied long-wheelbase models (the third was built as a full production vehicle) from an operator which was to become one of the Olympian's most important customers. With fleet numbers BL3 and BL2 respectively, these joined Kowloon Motor Bus (KMB) of Hong Kong. Despite their dual-door bodywork they featured seating for no fewer than 99 passengers thanks to their 3+2 seating arrangement, at that time considered acceptable for buses in the Far East, where the average passenger is rather smaller than in Europe.

With two prototypes thoroughly tested and nine B45s completed altogether, Bristol was ready to commence full production. Already a healthy order book existed, and it was becoming clear that with a little less sophistication than the Titan — and considerably more flexibility — the Olympian would be a strong rival for any of its competitors.

Above right: **When full production of Olympians got underway a further publicity brochure appeared which contained a range of Olympian photographs overseas, including several of the pre-production batch of B45s. Adorning the cover was a picture of B45-08, one of the earliest Olympians for KMB in Hong Kong, in which fleet it became BL3 (CR 2963).**

Right: **Exhibited on the Northern Counties stand at the 1980 Motor Show was B45-05, with a 75-seat body featuring a sturdy HELP bumper protruding from the front. Destined for Greater Manchester PTE as 1451, it was one of the few buses on display to carry its correct registration number (NJA 568W). Livery was the refreshingly striking orange and white inherited from SELNEC (and shortly to be replaced by a simplified version). After withdrawal in Manchester this vehicle worked for Black Prince and MK Metro but has since been restored to original condition by the SELNEC Preservation Society.**
M. S. Curtis

Bristol production

Production of Olympian chassis commenced at Bristol Commercial Vehicles early in 1981 alongside existing Bristol types, most notably the VRT double-deck model.

Type designations for production Olympian chassis followed contemporary Leyland practice, the first and last letters of the model name being followed by the engine type, a further digit (1 or 2) to denote wheelbase and finally an indication of whether the chassis was left- or right-hand drive. Thus a standard-wheelbase model for the British market, with Gardner 6LXB engine, was classified ONLXB/1R, while a long-wheelbase, Leyland-powered export model might be an ONTL11/2L. The letters 'ON' were also used to prefix the individual chassis numbers, commencing at ON1.

There was no shortage of orders, and the customer list was a fascinating amalgam of traditional Bristol and Leyland users. NBC subsidiaries would take the Olympian in large numbers as the natural successor to the VRT, normally with low-height ECW bodywork finished in NBC's corporate red or green liveries, the first production chassis forming the basis of one such vehicle, GFR 101W, which followed B45-02 to Ribble. Two NBC subsidiaries were encouraged to accept Roe bodywork, which was a little taller, being built to an overall height of 14ft 2in, and featured a curved windscreen which differed from the BET design that had become established on ECW-bodied Bristols; these were London Country, which already operated many Atlanteans (and a few Fleetlines) fitted with a similar type of

ON1, the first production Olympian, followed prototype B45-02 into the fleet of Ribble Motor Services as 2101 (GFR 101W), entering service from April 1981. It was an **ONLXB/1R** model with ECW bodywork. *Author's collection*

Below: **The original block letter badges, as applied to the earliest Leyland Olympians.**

Right: **Bristol Omnibus 9543 (NTC 142Y), a Roe-bodied Olympian finished in standard NBC green and white.** Delivered in 1983, it was photographed at Stockwood later that year, by which time Bristol's city buses had adopted the rather meaningless 'CITYBUS' fleetname. These vehicles were fitted with Transign electronic route-indicator equipment, which unfortunately was prone to display something other than the intended destination!
M. S. Curtis

Right: **The additional height of Roe's taller bodywork allowed back-to-back seating to be provided over the rear wheel arches.** This interior view from another of the Bristol batch demonstrates how a forward-mounted bench seat increased the standing and circulation area available for city passengers.
M. S. Curtis

Above: **Whilst 'Tilling' green livery had been superseded in England and Wales by NBC leaf green, it survived in Scotland with Eastern Scottish, where it was officially known as 'Lothian' green. Brand-new HH112 (ULS 112X) looks superb in this livery at Edinburgh's St Andrew Square bus station in April 1982.**
M. S. Curtis

Left: **Chassis ON217 formed the basis of Alexander (Northern) NLO28 (TSO 28X), which received 77-seat ECW bodywork. In this view in Aberdeen corporate 'Northern Scottish' fleetnames are in evidence — an acknowledgement of the fact that, like their state-owned counterparts south of the border, the Scottish companies were also part of a group. This bus is also fitted with SBG's characteristic 'triangular' destination screen.**
Author's collection

screen, and — more surprisingly, given its deep-rooted historical links with ECW — Bristol Omnibus, which had never previously purchased bodywork from Roe.

Some interest was also forthcoming from the state-owned Scottish Bus Group, which, following an unhappy experience with early Bristol VRTs, had been more wary than most of rear-engined double-deckers.

Early municipal operators, which might previously have ordered from either Bristol or Leyland, included Bournemouth, Derby, Cardiff, Lothian, Lincoln, Nottingham, Plymouth and Warrington, while substantial support came from the PTEs (from which Leyland had earlier hoped to win orders for its Titan), Greater Manchester, Merseyside, Strathclyde and West Yorkshire all placing orders. This group included both standard- and (in the case of the municipalities) long-wheelbase examples, with a variety of body designs produced by Alexander, East Lancs, Marshall and Northern Counties in addition to ECW and Roe, which builders' bodywork for this sector included versions with flat windscreens.

Perhaps the most concerted sales effort, which yielded some significant orders, was directed overseas, an area in which Leyland had a wealth of experience, and among the demonstrators built for various export markets were left-hand drive versions for the Middle East, Portugal and Greece, the last of which resulted in an order from Athens for a further 19 buses. The Olympian name was, of course, particularly appropriate here, and specially produced badges with the model name in Greek lettering were affixed to these vehicles.

By far the most important overseas markets were those in the Far East. For operation in Hong Kong, China Motor Bus took standard- and long-wheelbase Olympians, while Kowloon Motor Bus followed its initial long-wheelbase trio with chassis ON119, which formed the basis of a huge ECW-bodied, 39ft 4in (12m)-long three-axle vehicle (3BL1) incorporating three passenger doors while still providing seating for well over 100 passengers. This was the first three-axle chassis built by Bristol since 1929 (when the company produced its C-type motor-bus and E-type trolleybus chassis) and was followed by the similar ON332, which was finished in China Motor Bus colours. However, this was destined never to join CMB and, after testing, followed by extensive rebuilding as a coach, was eventually sold instead to Citybus for use on its service between Hong Kong and China. These vehicles were the forerunners of vast quantities of similar chassis for the

Bournemouth was an early customer for the Olympian, taking a batch of 20 which was unique in having Marshall bodywork. No 192 (TJT 192X) is pictured crossing the Square in May 1983.
M. S. Curtis

Left: **In March 1982 Lothian introduced two Alexander-bodied ONTL11/1R models — the first of a large fleet of Olympians, although all subsequent examples were long-wheelbase versions. Seen in Princes Street, Edinburgh, when still brand-new is 666 (GSC 666X).** *M. S. Curtis*

Below: **Having amassed a large fleet of Atlanteans, Plymouth City Transport introduced a trio of East Lancs-bodied Olympians in 1982, although no further orders followed. Rather than neatly enclosing the engine area, the bodywork featured a recessed rear window above the engine compartment, as apparent from this view of 174 (TTT 174X) in Royal Parade. Plymouth was among a number of operators to fit front wheel-nut guards, a long-established Leyland tradition.** *M. S. Curtis*

Right: **Cardiff also chose East Lancs to body its Olympians, which followed large numbers of Bristol VRTs. In this April 1987 scene 510 (RBO 510Y) is heading away from the Newport Road *en route* to the bus and railway stations.**
M. S. Curtis

Below: **Of the various styles of bodywork mounted on Olympian chassis East Lancs' was probably the most severe. Photographed in Lincoln High Street during July 1991, Lincoln 45 (KTL 45Y) was one of four long-wheelbase ONLXB/2R versions received by the operator during 1982.**
M. S. Curtis

Above: **Merseyside PTE bought a batch of 10 early-production Olympians which were fitted with the taller version of bodywork incorporating flat windscreens, built by Eastern Coach Works. Based on chassis ON41, 0033 (ACM 707X) featured Transdot electronic destination equipment. These vehicles were later joined by five more Bristol-built Olympians, with Alexander bodywork, and operated alongside Dennis, MCW and Volvo models for comparison purposes.**
Author's collection

Left: **Greater Glasgow PTE had been re-titled Strathclyde PTE by the autumn of 1981, when it began taking delivery of both Roe- and ECW-bodied production Olympians. Low-height ECW bodywork, with flat windscreens, was fitted to LO14 (CGG 837X), an ONTL11/1R model.**
Author's collection

Right: **West Yorkshire PTE rapidly became the biggest customer for Bristol-built Olympians, taking no fewer than 96. Here two early examples rest at Skircoat Road depot, Halifax. Although consecutively numbered, 5020/1 carry different styles of manufacturer's badging, having been built six months apart as part of different batches, with registrations from different series. The Roe highbridge bodywork provided seating for 76 passengers.**
Author's collection

Below right: **One of Leyland's strengths was that, over many years, it had achieved considerable success in winning export orders. From the outset of the B45 project tremendous efforts had been made to gain overseas business for the Olympian, notably in Hong Kong, where the two major operators each took early examples with dual-door ECW bodywork. Three long-wheelbase buses were supplied to KMB, while chassis ON16 and ON17 were allocated to China Motor Bus. The first of these, numbered BR1, was a short-wheelbase 89-seater, while the second, BR2, seen here prior to despatch, was a long-wheelbase ONLXB/2R, with seating for 99. The high capacities were achieved by virtue of a 3+2 layout.**
ECW

Above: **Chassis ON73 received a 78-seat dual-door ECW body to become a left-hand-drive demonstrator for Portugal, where both Atlanteans and Fleetlines had previously operated. An ONTL11/2L model, it would be registered TA-46-45 for operation with CARRIS in Lisbon. Thereafter it travelled to Brazil and Egypt but failed to attract any orders.**
ECW

Left: **ON52 was another ECW-bodied, left-hand-drive ONTL11/2L demonstrator, which achieved rather more success. It was sent to Athens, where it was not only purchased but followed by an order for 19 similar buses, one of which is pictured in service during 1983. Unlike the original vehicle the production batch featured deep sliding windows and Olympian badges in Greek.**
Mike Walker

Right: **While production continued at Bristol a great deal of technical development was undertaken to produce new variants. Shown on the production line at BCV's Chatsworth Road works during August 1981 is chassis ON119, the first three-axle Olympian chassis.** *M. S. Curtis*

Right: **Destined for KMB, the first three-axle Olympian, powered by a Leyland TL11 engine, was bodied by ECW (EX18). This enormous vehicle — the largest yet produced by Bristol/ECW — was 39ft 4in (12m) long, had three passenger doorways and, with the 3+2 arrangement, provided seating for 104. Taking into account standing passengers, it was approved to carry a total of 157 — double that of a standard NBC Olympian! Numbered 3BL1, it was given Hong Kong registration CV 184.** *ECW*

Right: **KMB 3BL1 operating service 80K to Sun Chui, having now received a brighter livery. Every one of its deep tropical windows is in the open position, reflecting the operating conditions in Hong Kong.** *Ricky Chan*

Above: **A view of the yard at BCV's Chatsworth Road works during May 1982. This chassis is ON332, the second tri-axle Olympian to be built and here fitted with additional framework for extensive testing of loads and body structure. It later received ECW body EX19, which was very similar to that mounted on ON119 for KMB but was finished in CMB blue and cream. It was never delivered, however, and at the time of BCV's closure remained at Bristol's Bath Road experimental shop.**
M. S. Curtis

Left: **ON332 eventually had its body rebuilt by ECW to produce a double-deck coach, though it retained its original frame, with shorter window spacing in the centre. It was then purchased by Citybus in Hong Kong (C51, later 102) and given registration DE 4281. Employed initially — from 1985 — on the cross-border services to Shenzhen and Guangzhou, it is seen here 12 years later in the role of advanced driver-training vehicle in Hong Kong's Central District.**
M. S. Curtis

Far East, most with Alexander bodywork which was supplied in completely knocked-down (CKD) form for assembly locally. By the autumn of 1983 Bristol would build two further batches for KMB, each consisting of 20 vehicles, of both its standard-wheelbase and three-axle Olympian chassis, the latter powered by the turbocharged Gardner 6LXCT engine. These three-axle chassis received the code '3' as their wheelbase designation.

Various vehicles acted as UK demonstrators, Roe-bodied West Yorkshire PTE 5011 (UWW 11X) even receiving a special livery for this role when new. In South Yorkshire the independent operator to run under this title purchased two 71-seat Northern Counties-bodied vehicles from the first year's production, to be followed a little later by South Yorkshire PTE, which took a pair of Roe-bodied examples diverted from West Yorkshire PTE.

More than 250 Olympian chassis had been completed by the end of 1981, by which time the type had completely replaced the VRT (which ceased production during August) to become the only double-deck model produced by Bristol. Of its single-deck chassis, the final LH types were also assembled at the end of that year, while the Bristol RE continued until the following year to meet the requirements in Northern Ireland. The Leyland National-derived B21 chassis continued to be produced in small but steady numbers, while one final model also to appear from Bristol was the B52, another chassis intended for export (under the Leyland name) which combined an Olympian forward section with a horizontal TL11 engine mounted under the floor at the rear. Two left-hand-drive versions were displayed in Portugal, where its similarities to the Olympian were promoted, possibly with the intention of producing this as a B21 replacement.

Meanwhile another significant Olympian chassis for the home market was ON281, which formed the basis of a 36ft 8in (11.2m)-long, TL11-engined coach for National Express, with a 65-seat ECW body (EX20). Completed during 1982, it was registered ADD 50Y (its originally intended mark, SND 50X, having been surrendered) and allocated to National Travel West's Bristol-based Wessex unit. It was followed by a number of similar vehicles introduced by NBC subsidiaries for commuter or inter-urban work and itself later passed to Badgerline before being exported to Hong Kong.

Left: **ON120 became West Yorkshire PTE 5011 (UWW 11X)** but was used initially as a demonstrator and painted accordingly. It is seen visiting Bristol Omnibus early in 1982, prior to the arrival of Bristol's own Roe-bodied Olympians. *Bristol Vintage Bus Group*

Below: **Sold prematurely when Yorkshire Rider declined to take on their leases, many of the Roe-bodied Olympians new to West Yorkshire PTE reappeared with other operators in the UK when only four years old. Six, however, were exported to Hong Kong to join the Citybus fleet. Nos 18 (DN 4435) and 14 (DN 1648) — formerly WYPTE 5057/62 (CUB 57, 62Y) — are seen in Kowloon in 1997, having been converted to open-top for use on evening tours.** *M. S. Curtis*

Right: **Chassis ON281 represented the next significant development of the Olympian as it formed the basis of a prototype motorway coach designed for high-speed running. Powered by a TL11 unit, it was bodied by ECW (EX20) and provided seating for 65, together with ample luggage accommodation at the rear of the lower deck. New to National Travel West (50) during the summer of 1982, it was photographed prior to entering service with registration ADD 50Y as part of its operator's Bristol-based Wessex coaching unit.** *M. S. Curtis*

Right: **The cover of a brochure produced to promote the Olympian double-deck coach.**

Right: **In 1985 ADD 50Y was rebuilt by ECW with more seating and a reduced luggage area and transferred to Bristol Omnibus (2350), where it was among the first vehicles to appear in Badgerline livery, in preparation for the division of the company. From the beginning of 1986 the new Badgerline company assumed control of Bristol's country services, along with operations in Bath, Wells and Weston-super-Mare.** *M. S. Curtis*

Left: **At the end of 1987 Badgerline sold ADD 50Y to the rapidly developing Citybus company in Hong Kong. Upon its arrival an air-conditioning unit was added at the rear and it was prepared for the cross-border route to Shen Zhen in China, entering service by the end of 1988 in a livery of bright yellow with lettering and logos derived from those of National Express! Numbered C101, it was given Hong Kong registration EB 1030.**
Lyndon Rees

Below left: **In 1991 EB 1030 was converted to open-top, its air-conditioning unit being removed and plastic seating installed on the upper deck, while new front panelling of Alexander design replaced the original. It remained part of the Citybus fleet, renumbered 7, and wore Peak Tramways livery for operation on the short link between the Star Ferry pier and Lower Peak tram station. Photographed while so employed during March 1997, it later reverted to yellow fleet livery for use on evening tours in Kowloon.**
M. S. Curtis

Above: **In 1983 four ECW-bodied Olympians joined seven Bristol VRTs in the ownership of the Atomic Energy Research Establishment at Harwell, which used them for staff transport. Finished in a livery of blue and grey, they were kept in immaculate condition but were not normally accessible to the public. FWL 779Y is seen at out-muster during September 1989.**
M. S. Curtis

Right: **Based on ONTL11/1R chassis ON492, TFS 623Y was built in 1983 as a travelling art gallery for the Scottish Arts Council. Bodywork, by Roe, was clearly based on Olympian bus frames although built to a considerably lower overall height. The vehicle is seen in original condition shortly after completion.**
Scottish Arts Council

Other customers for Bristol-built Olympians included the Atomic Energy Research Establishment at Harwell, Oxfordshire, which purchased four ECW-bodied examples. These joined Harwell's fleet of Bristol VRTs in the provision of its own staff bus services to and from the AERE site.

Perhaps the most unusual Olympian of all, based on chassis ON492, was destined never to become a bus, instead receiving a Roe-built pantechnicon body to the requirements of the Scottish Arts Council, which was to use it as a mobile gallery.

With production passing 500 chassis during the summer of 1982, and with still more orders being received, the Olympian had not only got off to a successful start but had rapidly earned a reputation as a design capable of meeting a wide range of operating conditions.

The name 'Leyland Olympian' was established and was promoted at every opportunity, vehicle badging reflecting this, initially using discreet block letter strips carrying the words 'Leyland' and 'Olympian' which was soon modified to include a new version of Leyland's classic script, following restructuring of the Passenger Vehicle Division to become Leyland Bus in March 1981. Front-wheel-hub badges changed from Leyland roundels shortly afterwards. However, there were many who were less able to accept that this title was appropriate for a chassis produced by Bristol Commercial Vehicles, which Leyland did not fully control. Indeed, BCV itself continued to list these vehicles on its chassis production register as B45s — a term it also applied to customer order numbers. Of more significance, however, was the procedure used to create these vehicles' registration documents, which resulted in many Olympians' being licensed

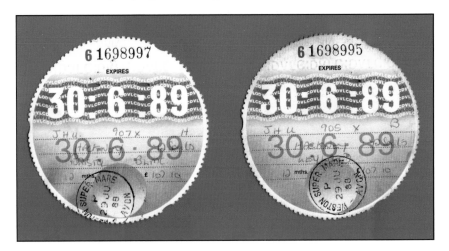

Above: **Wearing standard NBC livery, National Welsh HR860 (MUH 290X) departs Cardiff bus station during April 1987. Fitted with low-height ECW bodywork, it was typical of hundreds of Olympians introduced by NBC subsidiaries throughout England and Wales in the early 1980s.**
M. S. Curtis

Right: **Unusually for an NBC company, City of Oxford introduced Olympians with dual-door ECW bodywork incorporating a centrally positioned staircase. Here two Bristol-built examples pass in Cornmarket in April 1992. On the right, 220 (CUD 220Y) is still in NBC red, while on the left 209 (WWL 209X) has received a deeper red shade introduced when the company re-entered the private sector.**
M. S. Curtis

Left: **The Midland Red company was not an operator commonly associated with Bristol vehicles, yet under NBC Midland Red North introduced Bristol-built Olympians from 1983. In NBC red but with maroon 'Chaserider' branding, 1907 (EEH 907Y), a standard Gardner-engined vehicle with ECW body, arrives in Cannock when just a year old.** *M. S. Curtis*

Below: **Although NBC's livery policy was rigidly enforced, there were a few exceptions to the normal red or green. One such arose in the North East of England, where certain buses were permitted to wear yellow livery to co-ordinate with those of Tyne & Wear PTE. Built in 1981, Northern Olympian/ECW 3577 (JTY 377X) is pictured** *en route* **for Whitley Bay.** *Author's collection*

n Great Britain not as Leylands but as Bristols. As a result a significant number of Bristol-built Olympians for operation in the UK — indeed, possibly the majority — displayed 'Bristol' on their tax discs! Precisely how this came about is not entirely clear; certainly it does not seem to have been influenced by operators. For example, a municipal customer could find itself taking delivery of an entire batch of new Olympians licensed as Bristols, even though it had no previous history of running this make, while a traditional Bristol user might receive Olympians registered as Leylands. Some batches of Olympians to individual operators even comprised a combination of both manufacturers' names!

BCV's other joint owner, the National Bus Company, continued to order substantial numbers of Olympians, allocating Bristol-built examples to 23 of its 29 bus-operating subsidiaries, Bristol Omnibus, Crosville, London Country, Northern General, Oxford-South Midland, Ribble, United Automobile, United Counties, Yorkshire Traction, West Riding and West Yorkshire operating some of the largest Olympian fleets. However, NBC's annual reports made no reference to this new standard double-decker, despite the group's having recently conducted extensive Market Analysis Project (MAP) studies of its bus networks, which concluded that the role of double-deckers should be strengthened, with greater emphasis on local service networks. This was combined with the phasing out of the Government's New Bus Grant and a reduction in new vehicle orders overall, though demand for double-deckers and specifically the Olympian remained strong.

Morale of the workforce at Bristol was extremely high, some observers remarking that it was among the best they had encountered anywhere in the automotive industry. With very experienced and skilled personnel, it was the envy of many other manufacturers who were striving to achieve better staff relations and must have been recognised by Leyland management, with its own workforce in Lancashire similarly steeped in the traditions of commercial-vehicle building. BCV's main Bath Road works continued to comprise the experimental shop and also produced components, while chassis assembly was completed at its nearby Chatsworth Road premises.

It was, however, at Chatsworth Road that moves by Leyland to obliterate the Bristol name first became apparent, when a repaint of the buildings saw the removal of all BCV signage — a development recorded in the trade press at the time. In contrast, large versions of Bristol's scroll insignia remained at the main works.

Despite the Olympian's success, Leyland continued to struggle to win orders for its Titan and was losing market share across its remaining range of passenger models. Against this background it was perhaps extraordinary that instead of staging one of the largest displays — as it had at previous Motor Shows — Leyland Bus decided not to participate in the October 1982 event, leaving it to various coachbuilders to exhibit their products on Leyland chassis. This resulted in just one Olympian (for Greater Manchester) appearing on the Northern Counties stand.

Leyland did, however, continue to seek new business and attempted to win orders by offering 'whole-bus' deals to customers,

Above: **Maidstone & District was among the first operators to buy express-coach versions of the Olympian, following the appearance of the National Express prototype, ADD 50Y. Among them was 5441 (GKE 441Y), which received Invictaway lettering for use on services between Maidstone, the Medway Towns and London. Note the revised front panel introduced by ECW for its coach-bodied Olympians.** *Author's collection*

enerating controversy in Edinburgh here such an arrangement for ECW-odied Olympians prompted objections rom Alexander, the Scottish-based oachbuilder, which was clearly concerned bout its ability to compete for orders in uch circumstances.

Leyland also recognised the growing hreat posed by Volvo and decided to hallenge the Society of Motor Manufacturers & Traders (SMMT) and the

advertising authorities over Volvo's entitlement to claim its status as a British manufacturer, arguing that its components for assembly at Irvine, Scotland, were largely sourced outside the UK. This was an important consideration for some customers, particularly local-authority operators, which preferred to be seen supporting British manufacturers.

A month after the Motor Show, during November 1982, came another

Above: **Maidstone & District was among the first operators to buy express-coach versions of the Olympian, following the appearance of the National Express prototype, ADD 50Y. Among them was 5441 (GKE 441Y), which received Invictaway lettering for use on services between Maidstone, the Medway Towns and London. Note the revised front panel introduced by ECW for its coach-bodied Olympians.** *Author's collection*

Left: **Lothian followed the introduction of two standard-wheelbase ONTL11/1Rs with substantial orders for long-wheelbase ONTL11/2R models, which caused controversy through having ECW rather than Scottish-built Alexander bodywork. They were nevertheless fine vehicles and were always smartly turned out. Among the first of these dual-door vehicles, with seating for 81 passengers, was 670 (OFS 670Y), pictured at Tollcross in June 1993.** *M. S. Curtis*

announcement. Leyland Vehicles and the National Bus Company had decided to cease their joint manufacturing arrangements, Leyland having acquired NBC's 50% stake in Bus Manufacturers (Holdings) Ltd to give it complete control of Bristol, ECW, Roe, and the Leyland National factory at Workington. NBC cited recent financial losses as the grounds on which it wanted to withdraw, although it had moved far away from the position it inherited when formed 13 years earlier, when it closely collaborated with manufacturers and commanded considerable influence over bus design. Ken

Leyland
BUS

Bow Lane Leyland, Preston PR5 1SN U.K.
Telephone: 07744 24241   Telex: 67515

TO LEYLAND BUS EMPLOYEES
_____

I am writing to inform you that Leyland Vehicles Limited has acquired the National Bus Company shareholding in Bus Manufacturers (Holdings) Ltd which now becomes a wholly owned Leyland Vehicles subsidiary. The BM(H) activities will now come under the operational control of Leyland Bus which is already responsible for the day to day management of the four BM(H) factories; Bristol Commercial Vehicles, Charles H Roe at Leeds, Eastern Coach Works at Lowestoft and Leyland National at Workington.

In an increasingly competitive market it is felt that both the manufacture and operation of buses require single minded management attention to achieve the best results. Having reached agreement with National Bus Company on this point the logical route was to consolidate the jointly owned manufacturing activities into the Leyland Bus operation, leaving National Bus Company to concentrate on passenger services. The share transfer will make no difference to the close and harmonious relationship which has existed for many years. Indeed, by taking a step which contributes to the efficiency of both partners there is every reason to believe that a closer and more productive relationship will be fostered between the two groups.

This transfer in no way affects individual terms and conditions of employment.

W K MacIver
W K MACIVER
MANAGING DIRECTOR
LEYLAND BUS

Registered Office: Leyland Vehicles Ltd., Lancaster House, Leyland, Preston PR5 1SN   Registered in England No. 504772.

MacIver, Managing Director of Leyland Bus wrote to employees at Bristol, Leeds, Lowestoft and Workington to advise them of the takeover and to offer reassurance over their future employment.

Two months following the Bus Manufacturers takeover, Leyland announced its intention to close Bristol Commercial Vehicles.

Apart from the Olympian and the newly introduced Tiger coach chassis, Leyland lacked substantial orders. At Workington weekly Titan production was down to just five, while output of Leyland National single-deckers was even lower, at two per week. This compared with around 10 chassis produced each week at Bristol. Olympian production was therefore to be transferred to the under-utilised Workington factory, with components produced at Leyland in Lancashire, thus ending Bristol's 75 years of bus-building history. There was no opportunity for future employment for the 530 BCV staff, whose manufacturing skills would thus be lost.

A campaign to keep the Bristol works open proved futile, and the final Bristol-built Olympians rolled off the production line during September 1983. So came to an end not only bus-chassis production in Bristol but also the established practice of driving bare chassis on public roads. Every Bristol chassis was first road-tested and then driven to the coachworks, which in the case of Eastern Coach Works involved a two-day journey of 265 miles. Ironically a dynamometer had recently been installed at Chatsworth Road to reduce the need for road-testing, but hereafter all new chassis would be transported by lorry.

With plant and machinery already prepared for transfer to Leyland's Farington works, the final Bristol-built chassis, ON995, was driven out of the Chatsworth Road gates to commence its long journey to ECW at Lowestoft on Monday 3 October 1983. It was to form the basis of Devon General 1814 (A686 KDV), which entered service in Exeter shortly before Christmas.

Including prototypes and pre-production models, Bristol had produced a total of 1,004 Olympian chassis. And as the Brislington community was attempting to come to terms with the shock of BCV's closure despite a full order book, Olympian assembly was already underway at Workington.

Left: **Chassis ON995, an ONLXB/1R and the last vehicle built by Bristol Commercial Vehicles (note the commemorative board above the radiator), stands at the Bristol works on 30 September 1983. Over a period of 75 years some 37,000 chassis had been produced by Bristol, and, as would be the case elsewhere, the end of manufacturing here changed the character of the whole community. Just visible behind is a three-axle Olympian chassis frame, which would be taken to Workington for finishing.** *M. S. Curtis*

Left: **7.45 on the morning of Monday 3 October 1983, and, like thousands of chassis before it, ON995 is driven through the gates of BCV's Chatsworth Road works at the start of its 265-mile journey to ECW at Lowestoft. In the background the entire workforce have gathered to watch the departure of their final chassis. In keeping with tradition, the Bristol FLF (left) was being used to transport goods and staff, having been 'borrowed' from the 'operating department' — which, of course, was once part of the same company.** *Allen Janes / Phil Sposito*

Left: **By Christmas 1983 ON995 had received its ECW bodywork and had entered service in Exeter as Devon General 1814 (A686 KDV), being seen on 16 December at Lancelot Road while operating on service B.** *M. S. Curtis*

Right: **By the summer of 1990 ON995 had been transferred to Southern National (still as 1814), with which company it is seen working route 502 (although only two number tracks of its destination equipment appear to be working) at Weymouth.**
M. S. Curtis

Below: **ON995 moved again in 1996, this time to the Isle of Man, where it became 57 in the fleet of Isle of Man Transport and received new registration MAN 57N.**
Steve White

The Leyland years

Assembly of Olympian chassis at Workington saw numbering recommence from ON1001 (chassis numbers ON996-1000 being left unused). The first 15 Workington-built Olympians were for NBC subsidiary Crosville, with ECW bodies finished in standard NBC leaf green.

Bristol-built chassis No 814, which had been completed some months earlier for Crosville, had actually been sent to Workington upon completion rather than directly to Eastern Coach Works, so that it could be inspected by personnel at the Lilyhall plant. It was then dismantled and reassembled in order for staff to become familiar with its construction and, once rebuilt, was renumbered as Workington's second chassis (ON1002). At least one three-axle chassis frame was also constructed at Bristol and sent to Workington for finishing.

Very rapidly, Workington's version of the Olympian entered production, ensuring that the supply of chassis to bodybuilders was not interrupted. Nevertheless, a few teething troubles were encountered in the assembly of early Workington chassis, and, in a display of crushing insensitivity by Leyland management, selected personnel at Bristol were invited to visit Cumbria to offer advice. As these individuals had just lost their jobs, this request was, not surprisingly, declined!

From about this time, as part of a range of measures to reduce overall weight, the coolant header tank above the engine compartment was repositioned from the nearside to the offside, the position of the water filler cap therefore providing a means of visual distinction between Bristol-built chassis and those assembled at Workington. There were, however, a few exceptions: the second bulk order for Lothian, built at Bristol, already had coolant tanks in the new position, while conversely the first Workington-built chassis perpetuated the Bristol arrangement.

Another, very subtle identifier was also apparent on Olympians bodied by ECW. Sharp-eyed observers became aware that the Leyland grille badges were subtly different, those on Bristol chassis being cast

Crosville DOG131 (A131 SMA), with ECW bodywork mounted on ON1001, the first chassis built at Workington. It entered service during September 1983. *S.T. Sanderson*

Right: **Ready for delivery, three newly completed Olympians stand at Eastern Coach Works during the summer of 1983. The two in NBC green livery, destined for Crosville as DOG134/5 (A134/5 SMA), are based on Workington-built chassis ON1004/5, while the red bus, due to become Devon General 1805 (A681 KDV) has Bristol-built chassis ON928. They can be distinguished by the almost imperceptible difference in size of their Leyland badges, that on the Bristol-built bus being a cast version and fractionally smaller. Awaiting bodywork in the background are further Olympian chassis from Bristol.**
Author's collection

Below right: **Seen in Leicester in June 1989 is yet another vehicle from the early Workington-built batch for Crosville, A133 SMA (chassis ON1003), by now in the service of Midland Fox, a company created from the division of Midland Red. Its new fleet number was 4517.**
Author's collection

Bottom right: **Delivered to Bristol Omnibus in time for the 1984 summer season were six Leyland Olympians with convertible open-top bodywork by Roe. All were allocated to Weston-super-Mare, 8612 (A812 THW) being seen when still new, passing through the picturesque village of Uphill, on the outskirts of the town. Livery was white and blue.**
M. S. Curtis

netal versions, while those from Workington displayed almost imperceptibly arger, pressed versions (of a type already amiliar on Bristol-built chassis bodied by Roe). Somebody at ECW must have gone to considerable trouble to ensure the appropriate badge was applied to vehicles, s chassis from both locations passed hrough the coach factory simultaneously!

The National Bus Company continued to be one of the Olympian's major customers, generally with low-height ECW bodywork, although Bristol Omnibus and London Country continued to take Roe-bodied examples, the former's allocation including six with convertible-open-top bodywork for use at Weston-super-Mare.

Of those with ECW bodywork, Crosville, East Midland, Northern General, Ribble, United Automobile, Yorkshire Traction, West Riding and West Yorkshire Road Car amassed some of the largest fleets. Among new names added to the list of NBC Olympian operators in 1984/5 were Hampshire Bus, Lincolnshire, Red Bus (North Devon), South Wales and Wilts & Dorset, some of which were new or revived names, NBC having by now started to divide its subsidiaries into smaller units, reversing its policy of a decade earlier.

Wilts & Dorset was another early recipient of Workington-built Olympian chassis, five ONLXB/1R models, bodied by ECW and fitted with semi-coach seating, entering service in March 1984. This rear view of 3905 (A905 JPR), recorded at Salisbury bus station in April, illustrates how the ECW body had developed since the beginning of Olympian production; note the frameless emergency rear window (a feature first seen on Roe bodies), the offside coolant filler and the fact that the engine-ventilation grilles are now located below the waistband.
M. S. Curtis

Alder Valley, Eastern National, London Country (Green Line) and Maidstone & District each took into stock long-wheelbase Olympians with ECW's coach bodywork, while many other standard-length Olympians with standard body shells for NBC companies received coach seating.

Of the Scottish Bus Group subsidiaries, Alexander (Fife), Alexander (Northern), Highland and Scottish Omnibuses received early Workington-built chassis, all opting for Alexander bodywork produced at Falkirk.

Other early customers for Olympians assembled in Cumbria included the independent South Yorkshire concern, while the municipalities of Chester, Colchester, Eastbourne, Grampian, Grimsby-Cleethorpes, Ipswich, Northampton, Preston (whose first

Olympian, A33 MRN, with long-wheelbase chassis, acted as a demonstrator) and Southampton joined the growing list of Olympian operators. Among existing municipal operators, Warrington had two of its vehicles equipped with Maxwell transmissions, the first Olympians so fitted.

Of the Passenger Transport Executives, Greater Manchester and West Yorkshire continued to build up large Olympian fleets, each supporting its local coachbuilder – Northern Counties and Charles H. Roe respectively — while Tyne & Wear placed an order for 65 Alexander-bodied buses delivered in 1985/6. In due course South Yorkshire PTE also took one further Olympian, with a rather special ECW coach body (EX26). This vehicle, based on long-wheelbase, TL11-engined chassis ON1362, featured a revised design of front end which was more upright and, with deep windscreens, considerably more attractive than the existing design with raked-back windows at the front of the upper deck. Wearing the dark red and grey of Ebdon's of Sidcup, it was displayed on the Leyland Bus stand at the 1984 Motor Show — Leyland having decided to return to the event that year. However, Ebdon's declined to take delivery and, indeed, cancelled an order for two further similar chassis, so this vehicle was retained by Leyland until sold almost two years later to South Yorkshire PTE, with registration 4475 WE. The cause of the cancellation appears to have centred on seating capacity and weight: as built the Ebdon's coach contained 67 seats, a toilet

Left: **A rear view of another ECW coach-bodied Olympian, this time a Green Line vehicle new to London Country as LRC5 (A105 FPL) but by now 305 in the fleet of Kentish Bus. In common with all NBC's long-wheelbase Olympian coaches it was powered by a Leyland TL11 engine.**
M. S. Curtis

Left: **Eastern National adopted this delightful colour scheme for its commuter-coach fleet. No 4504 (B692 BPU) entered traffic in March 1985. Its coachwork accommodated 73 passengers and, unlike similar vehicles from other fleets, was of low-height design, with equal-depth windows on both decks.**
Author's collection

Left: **Having to some extent lost out to ECW earlier in the decade Alexander regained a monopoly of contracts for supplying double-deck bodywork to the Scottish Bus Group in 1983. This low-height body was built on chassis ON1098, the resultant vehicle entering service early in 1984 with Scottish Omnibuses as LL142 (A142 BSC). It was photographed at St Andrew Square bus station nine years later, by which time its operator had resurrected the SMT fleetname.**
M. S. Curtis

Right: **ON1070 was one of four chassis supplied to Grimsby-Cleethorpes, forming the basis of 74 (A74 GEE). All received ECW bodywork, but only two were fitted with centre doors and centrally located staircase, as here. Although the chassis was built at Workington, this bus retains a nearside coolant tank and filler.**
Author's collection

Below left: **Greater Manchester bought hundreds of Olympians with bodywork sourced from its local builder, Northern Counties. Pictured at Manchester Victoria station, proudly proclaiming its allegiance to Altrincham depot, 3158 (C158 YBA) had seating for 73 passengers.**
Author's collection

Below right: **A 72-seat, East Lancs-bodied ONLXB/1R, A209 DTO was new to Derby City Transport (209) but was sold in 1987 to Warrington Borough Transport, which had itself bought several Olympians new. It is seen smartly repainted in its new owner's colours, with fleet number 39.**
Author's collection

compartment and luggage area but in this form was found to exceed the axle-loading limit; to solve the problem a reduction in capacity was necessary, the vehicle finally entering service with seating for 63.

More coaches with similar styling were supplied to the rapidly developing Citybus concern in Hong Kong, while Olympian orders from neighbouring Kowloon Motor Bus now exceeded those from any other customer. Leyland was nevertheless competing hard in Hong Kong, where both MCW and, in particular, Dennis were fighting for a share of the market.

Another extremely significant order was that placed by London Buses for three ECW-bodied dual-door vehicles, with centre staircases and back-to-back seating over the rear wheel arches. Production of the Titan finally drew to a close during 1984, only 1,164 having been built — of which 1,125 were for London. However, before the last of these had been completed, London had introduced Olympians L1-3 (A101-3 SYE) as part of a programme of comparative trials that also involved two Mk II MCW Metrobuses, three Dennis Dominators and three Volvo Ailsa B55s, which were set to work mostly on route 170. The three Olympians were standard-wheelbase models but nevertheless included seating for 75 (compared with 68 or 70 in a Titan). Two had Gardner 6LXB engines, the third being TL11-powered, while both Hydracyclic and Voith transmissions were represented. All the vehicles involved were to be evaluated for up to two years.

Continued uncertainly was to prevail, however, Transport Secretary Nicholas Ridley introducing his White Paper 'Buses' during the summer of 1984. Little heed was taken of advice from those within the operating and manufacturing sectors of the bus industry concerning the effects this would have, for these were the years of the Thatcher Government which had a

Right: **ON1362**, the Ebdon's Olympian coach, as it appeared at the 1984 Motor Show, held at Birmingham's National Exhibition Centre. Eastern Coach Works' new front end and revised styling for this **ONTL11/2RSp** model undoubtedly looked impressive compared with the earlier design, but regrettably the vehicle was destined never to run in Ebdon's colours.
Steve White

Below: The same vehicle operating a school service eight years later, during October 1992, in Willsbridge, South Gloucestershire, having passed from South Yorkshire Transport to Swallow Coaches. Its registration had also been changed from **4475 WE**, initially to **C259 MWJ** and then to the highly inappropriate **253 DAF**!
M. S. Curtis

Above left: **Receiving attention outside Eastern Coach Works in September 1985 is ON1802, a tri-axle ONTL11/3R model with body EX19. Painted in a livery very like that used for NBC's express vehicles, it was intended as a demonstrator for Indonesia but was instead sold in 1987 to Citybus, Hong Kong, which added the vehicle to its cross-border coach fleet as C61 (DU 5866). Seating was provided for 78, along with an on-board toilet.** *M. J. Woolnough*

Left: **With the Houses of Parliament in the background, the first of London's three trial Olympians, L1 (A101 SYE), prepares to turn into Whitehall while operating on route 170 in October 1984.** *M. S. Curtis*

vision of a nation with bus services provided by dozens of small, privately owned companies, all competing for business. The proposals progressed rapidly to legislation which would drastically alter the structure of the industry with the deregulation of bus operations (outside London) and the break-up and sale of the state-owned National Bus Company and, later, the Scottish Bus Group.

With New Bus Grant now completely withdrawn, growing uncertainty created by Government policy resulted in fewer and fewer orders for new buses as bus managers questioned how confident they should be about the future of their businesses. Within NBC in particular, more subsidiary companies were being divided with the prospect that not only would they eventually be sold but that management teams might themselves be encouraged to bid for their own companies. Early in 1984 Devon General embarked on the wholesale replacement of large-capacity vehicles by introducing a fleet of Ford Transit

minibuses in Exeter. These were to provid high-frequency services which were no only designed to stimulate demand but als to deter competitors from entering th market. It set a trend that would shortly b followed by many other urban networ providers, further depressing demand fo new full-size buses.

Against this background Leyland' Ken MacIver again declared that there wa excess capacity in the bus-building industr as a whole — and addressed this in the usua way by announcing the closure of ye another production facility. This time it wa Charles H. Roe of Leeds, which company' coachbuilding activities would cease durin the autumn of 1984, resulting in 44 redundancies. Roe's production would b transferred to either Eastern Coach Work (in the case of double-deckers) o Workington (in respect of other work suc as coachwork for the Royal Tiger Doye model). Again, the effect of the closure o the local economy and community wa likely to be profound.

Customers that had previously supported Roe and continued to order the Olympian were directed towards ECW. In the case of London Country, deliveries continued to receive the operator's 'LR' (Leyland Roe) classification, and ECW went to the trouble of modifying its design in order for these to resemble earlier models with Leeds-built bodywork. Most obvious was the inclusion of the front dash, grille and more arched windscreen as included in the Roe design, although the side-mounted trafficators were positioned further back on ECW bodies, providing the discerning observer with a point of recognition; the engine-ventilation grilles were also rubber-mounted on ECW versions. Of greater significance, however, was the method of construction used by ECW, which resulted in flush panelling rather than the traditional method employed by Roe, with beading strips covering panel joints.

West Yorkshire PTE took a different path. Having amassed one of the largest fleets of Olympians while strongly supporting Roe for bodywork, it took further Olympians towards the end of 1985 but with bodywork built in ... Leeds! In an extra-ordinary turn of events, the workforce at

Roe had decided to use their redundancy pay to purchase the Roe factory from Leyland and re-launch the business as Optare. Among this company's first orders was one for bodywork on Olympians — using Leyland designs and some parts. Further, similar work was to follow while Optare was establishing its own range of passenger vehicle designs.

In the mid-1980s ON1410, a left-hand-drive ONTL11/2L chassis fitted with dual-door ECW bodywork was demonstrated across the USA and Canada, after which it was purchased by Gray Line, Victoria. In 1989 it passed to Brampton Transit, and is seen here in September 2008 displaying both its original British registration (B757 UHG) and Ontario licence plate BE7-347.
Stephen Cho

Meanwhile, at Leyland, efforts to find new markets for the Olympian continued, Leyland bravely attempting to break into the North American market by linking up with the Gillig Corporation of California and promoting a long-wheelbase demonstrator (based on chassis ON1410) with a dual-door ECW bus body (EX32). Initially registered in Britain as B757 UHG, this vehicle was built to comply with US regulations and specifications, including emission standards met by installing a 240bhp Cummins L10 engine, and at its launch in Washington DC during October 1984 it was announced that a city-by-city demonstration tour would commence early the following year. Gillig had plans to produce the Olympian in the USA, should orders for large numbers be forthcoming.

Orders for all types of large new buses were falling dramatically in the UK during this period. Leyland National production drew to a close during 1985, its replacement, the Leyland Lynx, not entering full production (at Workington) until later in the year. Orders announced by the state-owned groups reflected vastly differing requirements. The Scottish Bus Group continued to seek full-size vehicles, including some Olympians as well as examples of a new Leyland double-deck model — the Lion — which featured an underfloor engine (resulting in a high floor) and was being developed in conjunction with DAB, Leyland's Danish associate; significantly, it broadly followed the pattern of a rival double-deck model, the Volvo Citybus. NBC, meanwhile, was more interested in minibuses, ordering no

fewer than 1,000 Ford Transits for delivery in 1985/6.

During 1985 Government policy became law with the passing of that year's Transport Act. Deregulation outside London was implemented during 1986, causing many British operators to cease ordering new vehicles altogether or to restrict their intake to relatively inexpensive minibuses. The Act also made provision for the disposal of NBC (separate legislation following for Scotland). Accordingly the state-owned operators were to be sold off one at a time, Devon General being the first NBC operating company to go, so as some entered a new period of private ownership, others remained for the time being in the public sector.

These were bleak times for British bus manufacturers, but the Olympian managed to attract two significant customers. The first was London Buses, which announced an order for 260 Olympians to follow the three already on trial. These were to be Gardner-engined, with Hydracyclic transmission and again ECW-bodied, but incorporating a number of Ogle design features to allow easier access for less-able-bodied passengers. Modifications included a split-level entrance and lower exit arrangement with added step. A completely straight staircase over the front wheel arch contributed towards a reduced seating capacity for 68. The driver's position was also raised. Naturally, the interior finish was to London specification, but the whole body line seemed slightly higher than standard owing to the use of low-profile tyres (which was unique to this batch),

Left: **Seen in Nottingham in post-NBC livery, Trent 722 (C722 NNN) was one of its operator's final batch of four Olympians, delivered in December 1985. Fitted with standard ECW bus bodywork, it was an ONLXB/1RV model, with Voith transmission.** *Author's collection*

Below left: **One of a number of municipal operators to turn to the Olympian in the mid-1980s was Chester City Transport, which had previously favoured the Dennis Dominator. One of the first four, delivered in 1985, was 2 (B202 EFM), an ONLXB/1R with 75-seat Northern Counties bodywork. It is seen here manœuvring in the attractive village of Eccleston during June 2007, by which time its owner was trading as ChesterBus.** *Author's collection*

Below: **Grampian Transport selected Scottish-built Alexander bodywork for 10 new Leyland Olympians introduced during April 1985, among them 121 (B121 MSO) seen here. This operator formed the nucleus of GRT Holdings, which eventually merged with Badgerline Holdings to form FirstBus (later FirstGroup).** *Author's collection*

resulting in shallower wheel arches and deeper panelling than normal — all of which subtly changed the overall body shape compared with ECW's standard design. Fog lights were also omitted from a redesigned front bumper.

The second major order came from overseas, Singapore Bus Service requesting 100 Olympians to ONTL11/2R specification, with Alexander bodywork supplied in CKD form for assembly locally. SBS was an established Leyland customer, having previously purchased large numbers of Atlanteans.

Other limited orders for Olympians continued from a variety of sources. During 1985 the municipalities of Eastbourne and Warrington each received a pair of long-

Above: **A number of operators introduced long-wheelbase Olympians with East Lancs coach bodies, two such vehicles being C28/9 EUH, ONTL11/2Rs with luxury seating for 78 passengers. Part of a trio new to Rhymney Valley in September 1985, they arrived four years later in Badgerline's Bristol fleet, being seen posed here, freshly repainted, on Durdham Down.**
M. S. Curtis

Right: **After experience with the first batch of long-wheelbase Olympians, Lothian stipulated that the staircase be moved to a central position to improve passenger flow. No 743 (B743 GSC), a 1984 ECW-bodied ONTL11/2R, was captured at speed in Edinburgh in June 1993, turning from George Street into Hanover Street. The final bus of this batch (770) was bought back by Leyland to act as a demonstrator in Thailand and Malaysia before being sold to CityBus, Hong Kong.**
M. S. Curtis

wheelbase coach models with East Lancs bodies, as did London Buses, while that staunch supporter of the Olympian, Lothian Region Transport, announced an order for a further 24 ECW-bodied long-wheelbase buses.

Technical developments were also continuing, the Scottish Bus Group installing a turbocharged five-cylinder Gardner 5LXCT engine, developing 170bhp, in one of its Olympians. Meanwhile ECW-bodied chassis ON1600, fitted with a Cummins L10 engine and Voith transmission, became a Leyland development vehicle.

By the end of 1985 a new chassis-numbering series commencing at ON1000 had been introduced to reflect the fact that a second Olympian production line had opened at Farington — near the town of Leyland itself, in Lancashire. There were clearly sufficient orders to justify this, even though NBC subsidiaries had virtually ceased buying new full-size buses, for KMB in Hong Kong and Singapore Bus Service were continuing to place substantial orders, as was Greater Manchester Transport in the UK. Also received at around this time was what would be the only North American order for Olympians — 10 three-axle ECW-bodied versions — from Gray Line in San Francisco.

Left: **Kowloon Motor Bus continued to introduce both two- and three-axle Olympians. Alexander-bodied BL117 (DG 3734), a 1985 short-wheelbase example seating 93, turns into Waterloo Road, Kowloon, during November 2000.** *M. S. Curtis*

Below left: **The full length of a 12m KMB Olympian is demonstrated by this side-on view of 3BL151 (DJ 3644), with Alexander body, built in 1986. Full-depth opening windows and 3+2 seating complete the character of these massive people-movers.** *M. S. Curtis*

Bottom left: **Following the demonstration tour of B757 UHG Gray Line placed an order for 10 three-axle Olympians with ECW coach bodywork, and these were used initially in San Francisco. Among them was 602, seen in appalling weather conditions before leaving the UK, at the 90th-anniversary event held at Leyland during May 1986. Just visible behind is the 'Indonesian' demonstrator.** *Author's collection*

Bottom right: **Later several of the Gray Line vehicles were transferred to New York, and, in the case of this example, converted to open top. It is seen shortly after arrival in the city in August 1999, operating on Gray Line's sightseeing service with fleet number D237.** *M. S. Curtis*

Right: **Production of London's L class underway at Eastern Coach Works' premises during October 1986. By this time it was known that when this order was completed ECW would close down. Body production would eventually resume at Workington.**
M. S. Curtis

Above: **An ECW body plate, as fitted to each vehicle to leave Lowestoft (in this case London Buses L42).**

Below: **Rows of Olympian chassis for London wait their turn to receive bodywork at Lowestoft, having been delivered to ECW by lorry from Workington rather than driven from Bristol.**
M. S. Curtis

The still-to-be-privatised Scottish companies also allowed a limited number of new buses to be introduced, while a trickle of interest remained from a number of municipal operators — which were soon to be 'arm's-length' council-owned companies. A playbus was also constructed with Northern Counties coachwork to the requirements of Lambeth Borough Council, which on the face of it seems extremely extravagant, such vehicles usually being created from time-expired buses at the end of their normal working lives.

Despite the continuing flow of orders the uncertainty created by the Transport Act extended to manufacturers. Plummeting sales of large buses generally resulted in suggestions and proposals of mergers and takeovers, Leyland being at the centre of the speculation. Among those showing interest were overseas manufacturers — a situation which only a few years earlier would have been unimaginable.

During 1986 American engine manufacturer Cummins took over Leyland Vehicles' Self-Changing Gears subsidiary, whose gearboxes were built under licence by Leyland for passenger-vehicle use. By the summer bids were being invited for Leyland Bus, although it was not alone, as the Government was additionally seeking the disposal of other divisions of the British Leyland organisation, including Leyland Trucks, Freight Rover, Land Rover and Unipart. By August it had been announced that Leyland Bus would be subject to a management buy-out, which included the plants at Farington and Workington, together with its product range of Olympian and Lynx service buses, Tiger and Royal Tiger coaches and double-deck bodywork. It did not, however, include Eastern Coach Works at Lowestoft, which was to close following the completion of the contract for London Buses. ECW was Britain's largest passenger-vehicle coachworks, and, like other factories previously shut down by Leyland

Left: **Three Olympians destined for London Buses in the body-assembly shop at Lowestoft, as the end for Eastern Coach Works draws near.**
M. S. Curtis

comprised a loyal and highly skilled workforce with a long tradition of building a range of high-quality products. Under the terms of the deal it was to be the Rover Group (formed from British Leyland's car division) that would carry responsibility for redundancy payments.

Production at Lowestoft came to an end early in 1987, by which time ECW had completed 1,470 Olympian bodies. Once again it was Workington that stood to benefit, the intention being to transfer Olympian body production to Cumbria, although in this case the relocation would not be as smooth as Leyland might have hoped. In contrast, Olympian chassis assembly would cease at Workington, this work to be carried out entirely at Farington in future. Of 2,600 Leyland Bus employees, 1,250 would lose their jobs under these arrangements, including 500 personnel at ECW.

By the spring of 1987 more than 3,000 Olympians had been built. The British bus industry was still coming to terms with rapid and ongoing change of a kind never previously witnessed by operators or manufacturers, but the Olympian continued to attract orders sufficient to allow production to continue, in particular from its largest customer, Kowloon Motor Bus, which by now had more than 460 in service. Despite being surrounded by ongoing manufacturing uncertainties, the Olympian was well on its way to becoming one of the best-selling double-deckers ever produced.

Below left: **Several ex-London L-class Olympians have been operated by Bath Bus Company, among them C48 CHM (formerly L48), seen in 2002 in its new owner's then livery of London red with cream relief. The appearance of these vehicles was altered considerably by the split-level entrance and low-profile tyres.**
M. S. Curtis

Below: **Following service in London L68 (C68 CHM) was exported to Australia where it remained the only Olympian for several years. Operated by Bankski Tours of Payneham, with licence plate WWX 500, it was photographed in Adelaide during 2004.**
Scott Mitchell

Right: **The last of the London Buses L-class order and the final bus built by Eastern Coach Works became L263, with registration D263 FUL. However, it was soon re-registered with a former Routemaster mark, VLT 9, and for several years attended rallies and special events, being seen here in Plymouth in May 1990.**
M. S. Curtis

Right: **By now registered D367 JJD, L263 was withdrawn from London service in 2000, having worked latterly for Stagecoach East London. It then joined the fleet of Blackburn Transport, where it remained until 2007 before passing to Blackpool Transport as its 411 and acquiring a smart new Metro livery. By this time also it had been neatly converted to single door, as apparent from this photograph taken in the autumn of 2008.**
A. C. Field

Volvo steps in

With the closure of Eastern Coach Works during the spring of 1987 Leyland Bus was without its own bodybuilding facility for Olympian double-deckers. Arrangements were in hand to transfer jigs, tools and equipment from Lowestoft in order to resume production at Workington, but this would take time.

Several other coachbuilders were to benefit from this situation, notably (and somewhat ironically) Optare, which was permitted to continue building the ECW/Roe Olympian body design under licence. During 1987/8 orders were therefore fulfilled from the former Roe premises, which Leyland had earlier closed, for Reading Transport, Cambus, Cityrama, Boro'line Maidstone and still more for Yorkshire Rider, as West Yorkshire PTE's operations had become known.

Northern Counties of Wigan also attracted growing numbers of orders for Olympian bodywork — including from many operators that were previously subsidiaries of NBC and which might otherwise have purchased the ECW/Roe design. Alexander, meanwhile, was by now producing Olympian bodywork — including CKD kits for export — in greater quantities than any other coachbuilder, its R-type body proving particularly popular.

Potential development of the Olympian chassis was also continuing. A twin-steer version was designed for Hong Kong, while alternatives to air suspension were also considered for some markets. However, these particular ideas failed to progress beyond the drawing board.

Meanwhile control of Leyland Bus was about to change once more. In March 1988

Having previously chosen ECW bodywork for its Olympians, Reading Transport turned to Optare to produce a similar design, which included use of the ECW 'coach' front panel. No 15 (E915 DRD) stands at Mill Lane during December 1988 when still only a few months old.
M. S. Curtis

Another operator to turn to Optare for bodywork of ECW/Roe design was Cambus. In February 1988 it took delivery of three coach-seated vehicles, 500-2 (E500-2 LFL), the first of which is seen here.
Photobus

— just 14 months after the management buy-out — the British motor industry was stunned by the news that the management of Leyland Bus had sold the business to its arch-rival, Volvo. The impact of this was profound. After all the effort to maintain the business through economies, factory closures and redundancies, Britain's leading bus producer was now in the hands of an overseas competitor. This situation would have been unthinkable just a year or two earlier yet could be attributed directly to Government policies of the time, coupled with an inability by Leyland Bus management to adapt successfully to changing circumstances or appreciate the worth of its own personnel or long-established production facilities. There was dismay also from many operators, whose

support in terms of vehicle orders had be crucial to retaining Leyland's British b manufacturing base.

What was good about the news was th the buyer was Volvo — one of the worl most respected vehicle builders, and who product quality was well known. Initia Leyland Bus became a subsidiary of t Volvo Bus Corporation, Leyland outp continuing independently until furth assessment of its range and facilities co be undertaken. Output from the Lilyh factory included rear-engined Lynx sing deckers, while a significant number of st were also engaged in railbus productio (although this was coming to an end); t Royal Tiger Doyen was soon abandoned.

By mid-1988 Leyland was at last ready commence building the ECW/Roe-sty body at Workington. The first chassis receive a Workington body of this type w ON10686, with Cummins engine and transmission. This vehicle became demonstrator and appeared initially on t Isle of Man, displaying registratio BMN 88G. It was then loaned for trials wi Dublin Bus, during which time it carri Preston registration F817 URN, befo returning to the British mainland, and w successful in attracting chassis orde though not necessarily with Workingto built bodywork. It was eventually sold Solent Blue Line.

The Workington body was similar appearance to that produced by ECW b was soon modified to incorporate slight broader front corner pillars for the upp

Merseyside PTE had become Merseybus when this Northern Counties-bodied ONCL10/1RZ arrived in May 1988, by which date many other things had changed too. This is an Olympian built in Leyland itself, with Cummins engine and ZF transmission. Registered E201 WBG, it was numbered 201.
Author's collection

Left: **Early in 1989 OK Motor Services of Bishop Auckland introduced a trio of long-wheelbase ONCL10/2RZ models, among them F107 UEF seen here in Newcastle. Northern Counties built the 82-seat bodywork, which featured revised frontal styling that considerably improved its appearance.**
Author's collection

Below left: **With the demise of Eastern Coach Works Alexander regained its position as body supplier to Lothian Region Transport. No 823 (G823 GSX) followed the general layout of previous Lothian Olympians and offered seating for 81 in its dual-door bodywork. New in 1990, it was still in front-line service when photographed during April 2006.**
M. S. Curtis

Below: **In 1989 Suffolk-based H. C. Chambers & Son took delivery of three Alexander-bodied Leyland Olympians, the first of which was F243 RRT, an ONCL10/1RZ with Cummins engine and ZF transmission, new in February.**
Author's collection

Right: **The first Workington-built Olympian body, constructed to an overall height of 14ft 2in and with seating for 78 passengers, was mounted on chassis ON10686. It was employed initially as a demonstrator, being seen here while on loan to Isle of Man Transport, with IoM registration BMN 88G. Re-registered F817 URN, it later fulfilled a similar role in Dublin before being sold to Solent Blue Line.**
Author's collection

Olympian 9.6m
Double Deck Bus Body

NOMINAL CHASSIS DIMENSIONS

MODEL	A	B	C	D*	E
Line Height	2296mm	4963mm	2350mm	2462mm	4166mm
Normal Height	2296mm	4963mm	2360mm	2452mm	4318mm

* Over body.

TYPICAL BUS SEATING PLAN

One door, front forward ascending staircase, seating capacity 78

Lower saloon configuration, 31 seats, 17 standees.

Upper saloon configuration, 47 seats.

Leyland

Above: **Leyland publicity for the Workington-built Olympian body, available in both low- and normal-height form but in one length only, offering few variations on the standard design.**

Right: **Olympian body production in progress at Leyland's Lilyhall assembly plant at Workington, in February 1989.**
M. S. Curtis

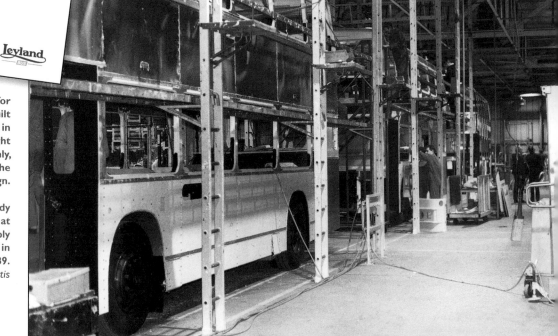

A view outside Leyland's Workington plant during June 1989. In the foreground, ready for delivery, are a number of Lynx single-deckers, including examples for Bristol City Line, while in the distance can be seen normal-height Olympians awaiting further attention before delivery to London Country North West.
M. S. Curtis

deck, resulting in a more upright leading edge to the foremost side windows. The use of the Cummins L10 engine (which by now had supplanted Leyland's own TL11 as the standard power unit for the Olympian) also caused the engine-ventilation arrangements to be revised. When Leyland came to construct the first such bodies, however, it encountered some difficulties in respect of the assembly of certain components. This appeared to be the result of a loss of knowledge between Lowestoft and Workington, which specifically related to aspects of the final production for this design. As a consequence, some bodies required further attention, and an early batch of vehicles for London Country North West remained parked outside the Workington assembly hall for some time until these matters could be resolved.

With the growing preference for Cummins engines (with power ratings of 180bhp, 220bhp or 250bhp) and ZF transmissions these units soon became

Delivery of Olympians to Hong Kong continued apace in the late 1980s, when KMB received these two 11m dual-door versions, seen at Kowloon station. On the left is S3BL231 (DV 8675), while on the right is S3BL188 (DR 3711). Both were powered by Gardner 6LXCT engines coupled to Voith transmission, their Alexander bodies each having a total capacity of 143 passengers, including 34 standing.
M. S. Curtis

Above: **Kowloon's Star Ferry terminal is a major hub of KMB bus activity. This night shot features three 11m Olympians — from left to right S3BL111/299/208 (DN 3426, DZ 483, DT 3269) — about to embark on new journeys. The two vehicles to the extreme right were built by Dennis, a company which competed keenly with Leyland for Hong Kong sales.** *M. S. Curtis*

Right: **Indicative of the investment made by Stagecoach, hundreds of long-wheelbase, Alexander-bodied Olympians were added to the group's fleets throughout the country. This example was new to United Counties as 639 (G639 EVV) in 1989, being seen when new in Midland Road, Bedford. Eighty-five seats were specified for the body, while Gardner's 6LXB engine remained the favoured power unit.** *M. S. Curtis*

standard, although many customers still called for Gardner engines. Leyland had now ceased production of its own power units and transmission, but occasionally Voith gearboxes were specified, the chosen gearbox type being denoted by a letter (H, V or Z) added to the chassis designation.

Huge Olympian orders continued to be received from the Far East, Kowloon Motor Bus and Singapore Bus Service between them helping to sustain output at healthy levels while the UK bus industry continued through its period of transition. There were the first indications too that the worst was over in the UK, British operators gaining confidence as they entered the private sector, encouraging some to order quantities of large vehicles once again. The Government's vision for many privatised bus operators was never to be realised, however, for market strength and economies of scale were to dictate that some of the first companies to enter the private sector would themselves bid for other concerns as they became available, and mergers and takeovers would also follow to form larger groups. The most dominant to emerge during the late 1980s were Badgerline and Stagecoach, each of which had a different approach to running its activities.

To the disappointment of many, Stagecoach swept away traditional liveries in favour of a corporate white with orange, red and blue stripes. Vehicle purchasing was also centralised, and as each newly acquired company joined the Stagecoach group investment in new vehicles usually followed, which invariably included Alexander-bodied Olympian double-deckers. By steadfastly supporting Britain's bus-manufacturing industry, the group

helped maintain the basis for future supplies, although the importance of this was perhaps not fully appreciated at the time.

The standard Stagecoach Olympian was the long-wheelbase version, but 1989 saw the introduction of a trio of high-capacity, 36ft 8in (11.2m)-long three-axle variants (chassis ON10898-900) with Gardner 6LXCT 220bhp engines — a type more commonly associated with Hong Kong. Two (each with semi-coach seating for 96), were allocated to Cumberland, while the third went to Magicbus in Glasgow; this example, branded 'Megadekka' and hailed at the time as 'Britain's Biggest Bus', featured the Asian-style 3+2 seating arrangement, which resulted in a total capacity of 110.

Badgerline followed a different approach, retaining strong local identities for each of its subsidiaries, and local autonomy allowed to the extent that even its depots followed different vehicle-purchasing policies. This is exemplified by Badgerline Ltd, the operating company formed in 1985 to run Bristol Omnibus Co's country services. Shortly after privatisation a fleet of new Volvo buses and coaches had been introduced at Weston-super-Mare, with engineering arranged on a contract-maintenance basis. The order included 12 double-deckers based on Volvo's underfloor-engined B10M Citybus chassis with perimeter framing, assembly of which took place at Volvo's plant at Irvine, in Scotland. However, when the next batch of new double-deckers was introduced for operation at Badgerline's Bath depot, the order comprised 10 Cummins-powered low-height Olympians to the requirements of local management. These were Workington-bodied examples which closely

One of the three 11.2m tri-axle Olympians introduced to the UK by Stagecoach in 1989, 'Megadekka' F110 NES (its registration deliberately chosen to reflect the fact that its Alexander body seated 110 passengers) was allocated initially to the group's Magicbus fleet in Glasgow. It was soon transferred south, however, being seen in the ownership of East Midland when just two years old.
M. S. Curtis

Right: **During September 1989 Badgerline took delivery of 10 low-height Workington-bodied Olympians for operation from Bath depot. Eight were standard service buses, while two were fitted with coach seating and specified with coach-style front dash panels, the moulds for which had to be retrieved from Optare. Posed here at Longwell Green the day before entering service are 9009 and 9004 (G909/4 TWS), representing the two versions.**
M. S. Curtis

Right: **The lower saloon of another bus from the Badgerline order, 9007 (G907 TWS).**
M. S. Curtis

Photographed in glorious sunshine at Ryde during August 1991, Southern Vectis 719 (G719 SDL), based on chassis ON11391, was another bus with an early Workington-built body, perpetuating as closely as possible the Bristol/ECW combination familiar in NBC days. The chassis designation had now become ON2R50C13Z5, indicative of Volvo influence. The inclusion of opening hopper vents in the first upper-deck side windows was an unusual feature.
M. S. Curtis

ollowed the established NBC approach to ehicle purchasing and could be considered irect successors to Bristol/ECW products. wo of this batch were finished to semi-oach standards, and to distinguish them rom the normal bus versions the company pecified the ECW design of coach dash anel — the moulds for which had to be etrieved from Optare, where they had last een used for a Reading order. Although ased on a well-established design, the Bath Olympians were not without their roblems, initially producing very high nternal temperatures in summer but reezing conditions for passengers and rivers in winter, to the extent that staff efused to drive them until they had been ectified. Such issues should never have risen in what was a proven model, and this vas yet a further example of how nowledge and expertise were lost as skilled ersonnel were shed each time production vas transferred between factories.

Included in the list of customers taking Workington-bodied Olympians were Isle of Man Transport, Colchester Borough Transport, A1 Service, London Buses, Preston, PMT, Metrobus, Viscount, Armchair, Southend, Thamesway, Capital Citybus, Strathclyde, Eastern Counties and Southern Vectis. It was a coach-seated example for Southern Vectis — one of several Olympians displayed at Coach & Bus '89, an exhibition held at the NEC — that betrayed the first small sign of Volvo influence. For decades many Leyland buses had displayed front wheel-nut guards, this being an attractive but solid device that enhanced overall appearance; the Southern Vectis vehicle at the NEC wore what was very clearly Volvo's design of wheel-nut ring, an embellishment with access holes to each individual wheel nut. It was a reflection that from about this time Volvo began to co-ordinate its own production and

Isle of Man Transport 88 (BMN 88G) turns at the Market Square, Castletown. Despite bearing the same registration this is not, however, the vehicle seen earlier in white livery but a later Workington-bodied bus which formed part of an order for six all-Leyland Olympians delivered in the latter half of 1988.
M. S. Curtis

A line of brand-new, normal-height Workington-bodied Olympians (with deeper lower-deck windows) at Basildon, awaiting entry into service with Thamesway — a company created by splitting Eastern National. Nearest the camera in this October 1990 view is 1003 (H103 KVX).
M. S. Curtis

Right: **Preston operated a number of Olympians (including second-hand examples) and, due probably to its proximity to Leyland, became involved with various demonstrators. This coach-bodied example, 107 (J107 KCW), was unique in the fleet, its Workington-built body being among the last produced, during the summer of 1991, and featuring unusual rectangular headlights. Note also the front wheel-nut ring, of obviously Volvo design.**
M. S. Curtis

Below right: **Equally unusual was this Eastern Counties vehicle, one of five with frontal styling similar to that of the Preston vehicle but built to lower overall height and fitted with bus seats. Photographed at Norwich bus station, DD25 (J625 BVG) was based on chassis ON20234, from the new 20xxx series.**
Author's collection

les efforts with those of Leyland, with the formation the previous year of L Bus & Coach (UK) Ltd. That the Leyland and Volvo ranges would increasingly be drawn together was demonstrated by chassis ON11140, which received Alexander bodywork and was used by Volvo as a demonstrator in Taiwan. was followed by a second demonstrator or Taiwan and another for Korea. he home market was catered for by a low-eight Workington-bodied demonstrator egistered G21 HHG, which was finished white and fitted with non-standard ectangular headlights.

In London the first steps towards the break-up of London Buses had been taken in April 1989 with the creation of 11 new operating units, with a view to privatisation. Contrasting with the situation elsewhere in Britain, the Government had decided to 'defer' deregulation of the capital's bus routes and to continue with the tendering process begun earlier in the decade. Thus regular orders for new buses would continue, many of these being for Olympians. In Scotland, meanwhile, privatisation of the SBG companies was proceeding under the provisions of the Transport (Scotland) Act 1989.

Although impressed with the Olympian chassis, Isle of Man Transport switched rapidly to Northern Counties for bodywork on its next examples, delivered in 1989, among which was 66 (BMN 66P), seen at Port Erin in 1994. *M. S. Curtis*

Right: **Northern Counties bodywork with a split-level entrance was fitted to this 1990 Olympian, Maidstone & District 5905 (G905 SKP) — a number difficult to miss from its roof-mounted position, intended to aid CCTV recognition. The modified livery is a vast improvement on the previous NBC standard.** *Stephen Morris*

Below: **In 1990 the first examples of an eventual fleet of 175 Leyland Olympians were introduced by Dublin Bus, with which this model was to become the standard double-decker. Bodywork was by Alexander, built not at Falkirk but at its coachworks in Belfast, Northern Ireland. Among the earliest was RH14 (90 D 1014), a standard-wheelbase ONCL10/1RZ model.** *M. S. Curtis*

Inset: **A Leyland Olympian chassis plate, as mounted in the engine compartment of Dublin Bus RH4 (90 D 1004).**

In 1990 a major new customer joined the ranks of Olympian operators when the first examples were delivered to Dublin Bus. This followed the earlier demonstration by ON10686, but the standard Dublin Olympian had dual-door bodywork built by Alexander at its Belfast coachworks in Northern Ireland. A total of 175 Leyland Olympians would be introduced by Dublin over the next few years.

Other orders were further strengthening demand, interest increasing from every sector of the UK operating industry, while in the Far East additional orders were forthcoming not only from Singapore but also Hong Kong, which was becoming of ever greater importance. The biggest customer remained KMB, which continued to take large numbers of tri-axle Olympians, as did Citybus, but the closing months of 1991 saw China Motor Bus (CMB) receive its first Olympians since its early Bristol-built examples. The Kowloon–Canton Railway additionally received 24 Olympians for use in Hong Kong, while China Light & Power took 15 examples, for staff transport, to be operated on its behalf by Citybus. By now new standards of comfort were being introduced, 3+2 seating being replaced by 2+2 arrangements and air-conditioning

becoming standard on new vehicles, ON10743, fitted with Alexander bodywork, becoming the first air-conditioned bus for KMB as its AL1 (DX 2437). Three-axle Olympians were built to produce overall lengths of 34ft (10.4m), 36ft (11m) and 39ft 4in (12m). An example of the longest tri-axle Olympians for Citybus, bodied in the UK by Alexander, was loaned briefly to Selkent and then to its intended operator's UK associate, Capital Citybus, for service trials in London prior to shipment to Hong Kong.

Above: **By the early 1990s standards for Hong Kong's buses had considerably improved, with the introduction of air-conditioning, sealed windows and 2+2 seating. KMB AL69 (EZ 1951), an 11m-long Olympian/ Alexander new in 1991, was among its operator's earliest buses built to this enhanced specification, identified by the mainly white livery.** *M. S. Curtis*

Left: **A small fleet of vehicles is provided by the Kowloon–Canton Railway Corporation in Hong Kong to provide feeder services. Among these are several Olympians, including 201 (EN 1504), built in 1990 with Alexander bodywork. The air-conditioning units for Hong Kong's buses occupy the area above the engine; as a result the route number has in this case been re-sited above the upper-deck window, in a position reminiscent of London buses of the 1940s and '50s.** *M. S. Curtis*

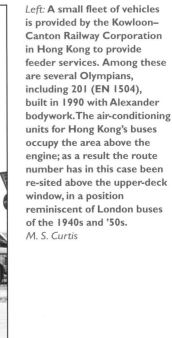

Many of the improvements in standards and service quality in Hong Kong could be attributed to the increasing prominence of Citybus vehicles. In 1989 the company introduced 12 11m tri-axle Oympians, powered by Cummins L10 engines coupled to ZF transmission, with Alexander bodywork incorporating 2+2 coach seating and air-conditioning. These vehicles were identifiable by their gasket-mounted windows (as opposed to the flush bonded glazing of later examples), as seen here on 109 (EF 1671).
M. S. Curtis

Besides the Olympian, Leyland's bus range still included not only the Lynx but also the mid-engined Tiger. By the early 1990s, however, these were gradually giving way to Volvo's own models, notably its highly successful B10M single-deck chassis. Volvo had embraced the Olympian, however, and even displayed a Workington-bodied example wearing London red in Stockholm.

Early in 1990 it was announced that Olympian production would again be transferred, this time back to Workington, spelling the end of Leyland chassis production at Farington. Perhaps even more surprising was that a new production facility for Volvo's B10M chassis was also to be established at Workington, supplementing output from Volvo's factory at Borås in Sweden. Production of both models at Workington would be based on a 'dock' assembly system rather than a conventional production line, Volvo believing that better quality workmanship and staff morale resulted from small teams of workers' building complete chassis. There was a double irony here, inasmuch as a similar approach had previously been employed at Bristol, where the Olympian was first built, while Workington had been specifically designed as the UK's first bus-

assembly plant to adopt car-typ production-line methods!

Olympian production duly resumed a Workington later in 1990 (in which year th sequence of chassis numbering, which ha reached ON11857, commenced a new serie starting with ON20001). However, the earl 1990s saw Britain entering an economi recession, and while closer integration o the Leyland and Volvo passenger ranges ha already taken place, general economi pressures continued to cause difficulties i the home market, prompting Volvo, whic continued to produce the majority of its UI output from Irvine, in Scotland, to conduct further review of its manufacturin requirements. The popularity o Workington's version of the Olympian bod had been disappointing, fewer than 20(having been built, while sales of the Lyn: remained limited. Late in 1991 th inevitable happened, Volvo announcing th end not only for the Lynx and the Olympia body but also for Workington itself, which i planned to close the following yea Remaining chassis production was to b transferred to Irvine — the Olympian was o the move once again!

The announcement that Workington wa: to close prompted all manner of questions otably whether it should ever have been established in the first place, whether attempts to support it artificially by transferring products from elsewhere had been justified, and whether any of the other long-established bus manufacturing plants, with their highly skilled, experienced workforces, could or should have survived instead.

In fact, Workington itself was to survive a little longer, for demand for the Olympian chassis remained strong, and in order to meet significant orders from both the home market and abroad production continued until the late summer of 1993; by this time the Olympian had become the last surviving bus model to bear the Leyland name. Customers to receive vehicles from the final year's production included City Line (Bristol), Bullock of Cheadle, China Motor Bus, Citybus (Hong Kong), Dublin Bus, East Kent, East Yorkshire, Keighley & District, Kowloon Motor Bus, London Buslines, Lothian, Maidstone & District, Sheffield Omnibus, Strathclyde, Southern Vectis, United Automobile and finally Singapore

Bus Service, which operator received chassis ON21080 (bodied by Alexander and registered SBS 9168S), the last Leyland Olympian of all.

By the time Workington closed a total 4,577 Olympians had been built by Leyland at its Farington and Workington plants (more than 2,500 of these, significantly, bodied by Alexander). Added to Bristol production, this made a grand total of 5,581 chassis, of which almost 1,600 were operating in Hong Kong or Singapore. However, the Olympian was far from finished; indeed, the most intensive phase of production was yet to come.

Alexander was to become by far the largest provider of Olympian bodywork. This bodybuilder's plate was affixed inside the cab of a Dublin example.

After a gap of more than eight years since its last Roe-bodied examples Bristol Omnibus turned to Northern Counties for its next Olympians, introduced in 1993, by which time a striking new colour scheme and rather anonymous 'City Line' fleetname had been introduced for Bristol's city services. One of a batch of 30, 9616 (K616 LAE) stands on the Downs, its livery incorporating a badger (over the rear wheel-arch) to indicate its group ownership. *Stuart Bond*

Above: **Citybus found it required a number of shorter (10.4m) vehicles for greater manœuvrability on certain routes, although the three-axle design was perpetuated, as their weight (including air-conditioning units) would otherwise have exceeded axle-loading limits. Among those delivered in 1993 was 231 (FS 3645), with CKD Alexander body assembled by KMB at Tuen Mun.**
M. S. Curtis

Right: **The tri-axle Olympian was also becoming increasingly familiar in Singapore, where similarly high standards were being adopted, leading to the title 'Superbus' being emblazoned across the upper-deck front windows. One of a batch of 200 placed in service in 1993/4, SBS 9056G, photographed here in October 2000, was authorised to carry a total of 131 passengers, including 38 standing.**
M. S. Curtis

The Olympian becomes a Volvo

Volvo's Irvine factory, established in the early 1970s, was primarily a truck-assembly plant, which built around 50% of the Volvo trucks for the UK market. It had also produced the Volvo Ailsa double-decker, a front-engined model which was nevertheless designed specifically to be one-man-operated. It included perimeter framing similar to that seen on Bristol Lodekkas and VRLs and, later, Leyland Olympian chassis.

Volvo's most recent double-decker was derived from its highly successful underfloor-engined B10M and when produced at Irvine, complete with a perimeter frame, was known as the Citybus. However, in the late 1980s production had been transferred to Sweden, where the Citybus name was dropped, the chassis modified to avoid the need for perimeter framing, and a new model designation (D10M) applied. Its underfloor-engine layout, whilst straightforward and reliable, required passengers to negotiate several entrance steps before reaching the lower deck and increased overall vehicle height, precluding its use by a number of operators.

The value of a low floor, coupled with the option of low overall height (as offered by the Olympian) was therefore well understood by Volvo, which was anxious to maintain customer loyalty upon the announcement that Olympian production by Leyland was to cease. Volvo Bus Ltd (as the organisation was by now known) wrote to all customers explaining the changes in its bus-assembly arrangements. The Olympian had become the world's best-selling double-deck model — and Volvo intended to keep it that way!

The Olympian itself was substantially 'Volvo-ised' upon transfer of production to Irvine, where a new purpose-built bus assembly hall had been created, and the docking system would continue to be employed. In fact the first prototype Volvo Olympian chassis, incorporating a range of modifications, had already been built by Leyland prior to the commencement of production in Scotland! Volvo engines were made available, the 9.6-litre TD102KF being offered as an alternative to the Cummins

A publicity brochure for the Olympian produced in March 1993, the Volvo name having now replaced Leyland, and the model itself now featuring a range of modifications.

OLYMPIAN DOUBLE DECK BUS CHASSIS

VOLVO

L10 unit (both meeting new Euro1 emission limits), with a choice of ZF or Voith gearboxes. In addition Volvo hubs, brakes and drums were introduced, together with a Volvo front axle, steering, electrical systems, air tanks and a B10M-type driver's binnacle. The frame continued to be of bolted construction, although the 'sticky bolts' introduced with the first B45s were no longer used.

From this point Olympians were known as Volvos, the first appearing on the road as the final Workington-built chassis were being completed. A new chassis-numbering sequence commenced at 25001, and a revised system of model codes was introduced, an Olympian chassis now being identified by the letters 'YN', followed by a sequence of numbers and letters indicating the number of axles, right- or left-hand drive, engine and gearbox type. (Some elements of this system had already been introduced for later Leyland-built chassis.) For a chassis bearing the Volvo name two features relating to the power unit were notable, the first being that the engine was mounted transversely (something the company had hitherto avoided), the second that a proptietary engine option was available.

Above: **Numerically the first Volvo Olympian, with chassis 25001 and type designation YN2RV18Z4, Capital Citybus 168 (L888 TTT) supports an early example of Northern Counties Palatine II bodywork (the first such body having been mounted on a *Leyland* Olympian for this operator). Northern Counties' more traditional body style also remained in production as the Palatine I.** *Author's collection*

Right: **Among the first Volvo Olympians to enter service were four for Western National which commenced operation during July 1993. They retained the more traditional Northern Counties body style, albeit fitted with coach seating. Seen in Paignton when only a few days old is the first of the batch, 801 (K801 ORL), on route X80 to Plymouth.** *M. S. Curtis*

Among the first Volvo Olympians to enter service, during July 1993, were four standard-wheelbase models with Northern Counties bodywork, delivered to Western National as its 801-4 (K801-4 ORL); powered by Volvo engines and ZF transmission, they were accordingly classified YN2RV18Z4.

Numerically the first two Volvo Olympians were introduced by Capital Citybus as its 168/7 (L888 TTT, L888 YTT), having received Northern Counties' stylish new Palatine II body, the first example of which had been mounted on this operator's final Leyland Olympian, 166 (K888 TKS). Several other early chassis were regarded as pre-production models and used for test purposes, some never receiving bodywork.

Orders already received ensured that the Volvo Olympian got off to a healthy start. Early customers included Blackpool, Bristol City Line, Bullock, Delaine, Gemsam (the holding company for Liverbus and London Suburban), Kelvin Central, London & Country, Lothian, Maidstone & District, Northumbria, Nottingham, Rossendale, Stagecoach, Strathclyde, Yorkshire Coastliner and Yorkshire Rider, while the chassis-order register also shows others were built for stock in the UK. Many of these customers' names were familiar, while some had been formed from the former state-owned companies, and others were new entrants to the market. Almost all were now in private ownership.

London continued to receive large numbers of Olympians, although no longer were these to a standardised design, for each company now selected its own bodybuilder and internal layout, subject to certain parameters dictated by the tendering regime. Early London customers included CentreWest, London Central, London United and Selkent (the last by now part of Stagecoach).

Other customers included council-owned companies, in many cases after a period when no new buses had entered their respective fleets, while also appearing on the order-sheets were the names of new independent companies, some of which had won London contracts.

In Ireland, Dublin Bus remained loyal to the Olympian, while strong support for the model continued to come from the Far East, Citybus, KMB and Singapore Bus Service continuing to purchase three-axle variants. More than 500 chassis were produced in the first year at Irvine, and this was set to rise significantly. By the mid-1990s Volvo was established as the largest producer of buses and coaches in Britain, and production capacity was increased still further at Irvine, Olympian output exceeding an astonishing 1,000 chassis per year.

A Mk II version of the Volvo Olympian was by this time being promoted, following further development, although the fundamental design remained as before, with Volvo or Cummins power units and overall lengths remaining at 31ft 5in (9.6m) or 33ft 8in (10.3m) for two-axle chassis and 34ft (10.4m), 37ft (11.3m) or 39ft 4in (12m) for tri-axle versions. With so many Olympians operating in the Asian climate, provision for air-conditioning units driven by the engine, with a power take-off from the gearbox, was an important feature for customers in the Far East. Finally, the adjustable steering wheel further added to driver comfort, which had always been very good.

Left: **In 1994/5 China Motor Bus introduced 30 11m Volvo Olympians with 104-seat dual-door Alexander bodywork featuring air-conditioning, by now regarded as *de rigueur*. No VA21 (GF 8579) was photographed operating cross-harbour tunnel service 112, being seen amid heavy traffic on the tunnel approach.** *M. S. Curtis*

Left: **In 1995 London United introduced a fleet of long-wheelbase Alexander Royale-bodied vehicles for Airbus services, with extensive luggage areas downstairs and most of the seating (43 seats out of 52) being confined to the upper deck. No A115 (N115 UHP) was captured at Heathrow in 2001. The Royale body design was derived from that supplied to Singapore.** *M. S. Curtis*

Left: **The A1 Service (Ayrshire Bus Owners) co-operative sold out to Stagecoach early in 1995, and shortly afterwards no fewer than 21 Cummins-powered, Alexander-bodied 79-seat Olympians arrived, among them N854 VHH. Unusually, the A1 livery was maintained for the main A1 route between Kilmarnock and Ardrossan in order to retain passenger goodwill.** *Author's collection*

Right: **Alexander's Royale bodywork offered a more refined appearance compared to the company's standard R type, and when finished in high-quality liveries such as that of East Yorkshire Motor Services looked most impressive. East Yorkshire was among very few companies to retain its independence following disposal by the National Bus Company, in February 1987. No 599 (N599 BRH) is pictured at Bridlington during August 2008.** *Author's collection*

Below right: **A shorter YN2RC16V3 model with Northern Counties bodywork, Stagecoach Selkent 327 (N327 HGK) was photographed as the doors closed at Westminster Bridge on a wet day in May 1996.** *M. S. Curtis*

Below: **The chassis-identification plate of a Volvo Olympian, Stagecoach Selkent 342 (N342 HGK). Note that the Cummins L10 engine fitted is described as a TDC100, implying a Volvo unit!**

VOLVO BUS LTD		
T.A.NO		
CHASS/VIN	*YV3YNC216SC026178*	
GVW	16800	17000
AXLE WTS 1	6300	6500
2	10500	11000
3		
	COUNTRY OF REGISTRATION	DESIGN
VEH TYPE	YN2RC16U3	
ENG TYPE	TDC100GA	

Left: **Not all London-area operators adopted standard red livery, and before such matters were controlled by the terms of tender contracts various colour schemes were in evidence. In this wintry scene P825 SGP, a Northern Counties-bodied Volvo Olympian wears the blue and yellow of Metrobus, operating routes in South East London.** *Author's collection*

Left: **During 1996 CentreWest introduced 15 Olympians with Northern Counties Palatine II bodywork for express route 607. Uxbridge Buses fleetnames were displayed from new, as was additional white relief, but V43 (P243 UCW) had also acquired First insignia by the time it was photographed heading towards Shepherd's Bush Green in November 1999.** *Author's collection*

Below left: **Northern Counties bodybuilder's plate.**

Pending the introduction from 1996 of Euro2 emission limits Volvo modified its engines to comply with the new requirements, while shortly afterwards Cummins engine options were dropped altogether upon withdrawal of the L10 unit.

By the end of 1997 more than 3,000 Volvo Olympians had been built, chassis numbers having reached the 28xxx range. By thi time the deletion of the Cummins engine and Voith transmission options allowed the chassis designation to be simplified to 'OLY-' followed by a two-digit number (typically 50 or 56 for the UK market and 65 or 72 for the Far East) to signify wheelbase.

Above: **Among the last Olympians delivered with a Cummins L10 engine was Dublin Bus RA294 (96 D 294), which entered service in City Swift livery. It is seen at speed when new in July 1996.**
M. S. Curtis

Right: **Capital Citybus was absorbed by First during July 1998, following which a predominantly red livery — but with strong yellow relief — was adopted throughout the fleet (together with First Capital fleetnames) in order to comply with a new ruling that London buses should be 80% red. No 227 (P227 MPU), with Alexander (Belfast), bodywork was one of 16 such vehicles required to work route 91 and is seen entering Trafalgar Square from the Strand.**
M. S. Curtis

Left: **Lothian followed Alexander-bodied Leyland Olympians with Alexander-bodied Volvo Olympians. Latterly, these featured Royale bodywork, represented here by 279 (P279 PSX), an 81-seater built in 1997. The photograph also serves to demonstrate how indiscriminate parking at bus stops can cause disruption and even danger for boarding passengers.** *Stephen Morris*

Below: **Alexander bodywork could also be found on long-wheelbase Olympians in London, among them this OLY-56, VA148 (R148 EVX) in Stagecoach's East London fleet, pausing at Bishopsgate. The dual-door layout allowed seating for 79.** *M. S. Curtis*

The grouping of British operators was still developing. Stagecoach, with its corporate livery, remained the most prominent, while during 1995 Badgerline merged with GRT Holdings (originally Grampian Regional Transport) to form FirstBus (later known as FirstGroup and nowadays trading simply as First); initially it allowed its subsidiaries to retain their individual identities but by 1997 was slowly introducing corporate colours and vehicle types — and seemed far less committed to double-deck operation than did many other operators. Cowie, having taken over British Bus, was also emerging as an important group, and as the gradual merging of operators continued, much of the individuality of companies disappeared.

In the Asian markets of Singapore and Hong Kong interest remained strong; in the case of the latter the impending handover (on 1 July 1997) of the colony from Britain to China seemed to prompt a concerted effort to buy as many new vehicles as possible prior to the change in control, although sales of British buses to Hong Kong have remained buoyant. In addition to the three main operators more Volvo Olympians were purchased by China Light & Power (2) and the Kowloon–Canton Railway (15). A further 15 were added to the fleet of Long Win for use on Airbus services, two went to HK Air Cargo and six to Stagecoach Hong Kong, which would later own Citybus for a period.

Alexander remained the main producer of Olympian bodywork, the only competition now coming from East Lancs and Northern Counties. Due to high demand Northern Counties became a second supplier to Hong

Brand-new City Line Volvo Olympian/Northern Counties 9663 (R663 NHY) stands gleaming at Bristol's Park Estate shortly after entering service in December 1997. Behind is 14-year-old Bristol-built Leyland Olympian/Roe 9549 (A949 SAE). Both have fleetnames in FirstGroup style; however, 9663 was one of four similar vehicles rapidly repainted into First's new corporate colours. *M. S. Curtis*

Kong, although in this market its products were badged as Plaxton, which was now in common ownership.

Interest in the Olympian started to wane from around 1998, owing to the introduction of a new range of vehicles with ultra-low floors rather than a step entrance as found on the Olympian, as this allowed faster and easier access for passengers. Indeed, the first low-floor double-deckers for the UK market, including a new model from Volvo, had been on display at the Coach & Bus show held at the NEC during October 1997.

1998 was also the year Volvo Bus Corporation announced plans to restructure and expand its operations in Europe, which would result in the eventual closure of the Irvine plant in favour of bus production outside the UK. This time, however, there would be no transfer of Olympian production, as ahead of the Irvine closure new models would be introduced to meet the ever-changing operating and market conditions. Olympian chassis production finally drew to a close during 1999, the last examples

entering service the following summer, 20 years after the first B45 prototypes had been unveiled.

The final Olympian for the UK market was delivered to Yorkshire Coastliner in August 2000 as its 437 (W437 CWX). It was the last of seven similar buses and, in common with the rest of the batch, was transferred in later life to First Somerset & Avon, operating from Bath depot. As such it regularly passed the author's house during the production of this book, running along the A4 trunk road to and from Bristol — the same road used by the earliest B45 and Olympian chassis on their test and delivery runs.

The honour of having the last Olympians of all rests with Irish operators. In terms of chassis numbers the Yorkshire Coastliner batch was followed by two final examples, Nos 29748/9, which were delivered to two Dublin-area independents, McConn and Morton respectively. However, it was Dublin Bus itself which claims to have placed the last new Olympian *into service* when its RV630 (99 D 630) entered traffic during October 2000, the last of 640 Olympians to be introduced by the operator.

Above: **Stanley, with its thriving market and beaches, is a popular destination for tourists on Hong Kong Island. Its small bus station is served by various Citybus services with additional bus stops, as here, alongside the main terminus. Here Volvo-powered 902 (GV 397), an 11m-long tri-axle model delivered in 1996 with Alexander bodywork, pauses while working route 260 between this attractive district and Central.**
M. S. Curtis

Right: **In order to meet demand for new vehicles in the period before the handover of Hong Kong to China some Olympians for Citybus were supplied with Northern Counties bodywork — badged as Plaxton, which had taken control of Northern Counties from 1995. A 12m vehicle delivered in October 1996, 504 (GX 7008) displays both Volvo and Plaxton names on its front panel as it heads for Cheung Sha Wan on cross-harbour route 171.**
M. S. Curtis

The biggest customer for the Volvo Olympian had been Kowloon Motor Bus, which ultimately received no fewer than 894, and this figure, added to the Leyland- and Bristol- built examples, gave KMB a grand total of 1,800, making it comfortably the most important Olympian customer overall. In Singapore SBS eventually received 571 Volvo Olympians, these outnumbering by some margin the 400 Leyland versions it had already placed in service.

In comparison with the Far East most Volvo Olympian fleets in the British Isles were modest: the Stagecoach group as a whole took 770, Dublin Bus 465, Lothian 434 and Strathclyde (latterly as part of

FirstGroup) 124, while the combined total for the main London operators (including 230 for Stagecoach) was 648.

Production of the Volvo Olympian was undertaken at a much higher rate than had been the case with the Leyland version, the number built between 1993 and 1999 totalling 4,717. Adding this figure to that of Bristol and Leyland gives a grand total of 10,298, of which more than 3,600 were exported to the Far East. The Olympian had survived a succession of difficulties in both the operating and manufacturing industries, to become one of the highest-volume bus models ever produced in the UK.

The Star Ferry Terminal at Central, at the opposite end of route 260, plays host to 11m Olympian 961 (HR 2697) on an express departure to Stanley.
M. S. Curtis

Above: **London Central NV64 (R264 LGH), a 1997 standard-wheelbase, Northern Counties-bodied 74-seater, on a rail-replacement service at Victoria.**
M. S. Curtis

Right: **Rather more severe bodywork was built by East Lancs, including this Pyoneer mounted on chassis 28468 to produce Nottingham City Transport 473 (R473 RRA).**
Author's collection

Left: **Sovereign Bus & Coach was created from a section of London Country (North East), later becoming part of the Blazefield group, which took over Borehamwood-based BTS to form Sovereign (London). Seen at Edgware station in its owner's very attractive colour scheme is the latter's 63 (S63 WNM), a Northern Counties-bodied Volvo Olympian built late in 1998.** *M. S. Curtis*

Below: **With the break-up of London Buses each newly formed London operator began to establish its own vehicle-purchasing policy while also adopting a range of livery variations. London United VA40 (R940 YOV), an OLY-50 model with 72-seat, dual-door Alexander bodywork was delivered in the summer of 1998, being seen here prior to entering service.** *Author's collection*

Olympian — Bristol • Leyland • Volvo

Above: **Among the later deliveries of Alexander-bodied Volvo Olympians to KMB was AV459 (HT 2699), seen here picking up passengers for Kwun Tong on route 101 in the Whanchai district of Hong Kong Island in November 2000.**
M. S. Curtis

Right: **The driver of a Singapore Volvo Olympian/ Alexander leans severely to his left as his mount, SBS 9625P, takes a corner at considerable speed. This vehicle was among the last batch of Olympians for this operator, supplied with CKD coachwork, placed in service late in 1999. It was photographed a year later.**
M. S. Curtis

Above: **The final Olympian for the UK market was a long-wheelbase Alexander Royale-bodied example (chassis 29747), which joined Blazefield subsidiary Yorkshire Coastliner as 437 (W437 CWX) in August 2000. This splendid view shows it when new, posed above Whitby.** *Stephen Morris*

Left: **Interior view of the upper deck of W437 CWX, showing high standards of passenger comfort as well as the seat-mounted grab-rails and stanchions.**
Stephen Morris

Olympian — Bristol • Leyland • Volvo

Above: **The same bus during the summer of 2006, by which time it had passed to First Somerset & Avon as No 34110. Photographed at Longwell Green, it is heading towards Keynsham on route 318.**
M. S. Curtis

Right: **The Olympian was popular with every sector of the bus industry, including established independents, with which Volvo had an excellent relationship. The final two Olympians built were both bought by Irish independents, the penultimate example, with East Lancs bodywork, going to McConn (trading as Dualway) of Rathcoole, registered 00 D 43135.**
Dualway

Reflections — and Super Olympians

More than a quarter of a century has now passed since the events leading to the Olympian's introduction, and when reflecting on the situation then prevailing one is still left stunned by the short-sighted approach adopted by Leyland's management. In their quest to save Leyland Bus in the short term they shut down BCV after it had — in remarkably little time — created the B45. This included the development by Bristol of a variety of Olympian variants for home and overseas. Leyland then closed Roe and ECW, each with a high skill base, traditions and the capability to 'build anything' from a body viewpoint. It kept Workington on the grounds that it was the most modern factory — but arguably with the wrong people, in the sense that in many cases they lacked the skills and abilities which had existed elsewhere. Furthermore, Leyland's bus management failed to recognise both the requirements of their customers, and the importance of their own personnel.

BCV, ECW and Roe — and Leyland's own historic works — were all capable of designing, building and developing models, whilst Workington's role was fundamentally an assembly shop for designs from other locations. The approach taken, when combined with Government policy of the day which itself seriously cut orders for new buses, left the Leyland bus group decimated. And once the decline had begun it became too difficult to halt.

All the benefits accruing from this situation fell into the hands of Volvo, whose Irvine plant had the required versatility to

Representing hundreds of Olympians in service with Stagecoach subsidiaries is this long-wheelbase Leyland model, about to depart Kingswear, with the River Dart behind, one evening in September 2008. No 14180 (G180 JHG) started life with Ribble in 1989 before being transferred to Cumberland and eventually to Devon. *M. S. Curtis*

design, develop and assemble trucks and buses. Today Volvo has replaced Leyland as market-leader in the UK and in many other world markets. Of the manufacturers listed near the beginning of Chapter 1, the only surviving builder of British double-deckers is Dennis — which, significantly, was never drawn into the Leyland web.

Optare also continues to survive — and thrive. Created from the Charles H. Roe bodybuilding business where there was a determination not to allow the skills and facilities to fade away, it serves to illustrate how a different course might have been taken by Leyland.

Throughout the Olympian's production life, demand remained sufficiently strong for it to survive — almost against the odds — as it was the right bus for its time. However, the events surrounding it offer important lessons. Whilst many believed that the policies of the 1980s injected new life into the operating industry, under the surface components within its very fabric were being destabilised. Much of the UK's bus-

manufacturing industry has disappeared as a result of the uncertainties then created.

The Olympian's production run also coincided with a period during which large concerns were broken up, only for them to re-form at the earliest opportunity as new larger groups. Stagecoach and First remain prominent transport providers, with interests that have expanded into railways and overseas. The Cowie organisation was renamed Arriva from 1997, and vehicles from all three groups now wear corporate livery styles — except in London, where red remains the standard colour for all buses. Go-Ahead has become a substantial, fourth group of operating companies, and alone encourages its subsidiaries to retain local names and identities. All these groups continue to run Olympians, although numbers are steadily diminishing.

A handful of former municipalities remain in council ownership, while a number are now owned wholly or in part by Transdev, Veolia or Kéolis. Through either banking or railway shareholdings these

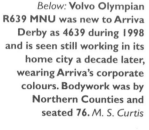

Below: **Volvo Olympian R639 MNU was new to Arriva Derby as 4639 during 1998 and is seen still working in its home city a decade later, wearing Arriva's corporate colours. Bodywork was by Northern Counties and seated 76.** *M. S. Curtis*

Among dozens of Olympians converted for open-top tour work is N537 LHG, now 307 in the fleet of Ensignbus and seen operating for the latter's Bath Bus Company subsidiary. It was built in 1996 for London Central (NV37), being one of many Volvo Olympians introduced to the capital in the mid-1990s. *Steve Pritchard*

There can be few operators of double-deckers in the UK that have not at some time run Olympians. A wide variety have appeared in the fleet of Bristol-based ABus, including B899 UAS, a standard-wheelbase Leyland ONLXB/1R with 77-seat Alexander bodywork. New to Highland as J15, it is pictured at the 2009 Glastonbury Festival, which event saw Olympians from operators large and small involved in the carriage of tens of thousands of music-lovers to and from the festival site. *M. S. Curtis*

Olympian — Bristol • Leyland • Volvo

three are owned, ultimately, by the French Government, while most recently Arriva has sold out to Deutsche Bahn, Germany's state-owned rail operator; it is impossible to escape the irony of a situation whereby many of the UK's former publicly-owned fleets now find themselves back in the state sector — albeit that of another country! The benefits and consequences of a return to private ownership continue to be debated, but the mechanism to prevent a complete removal of public services seems to have been largely eroded. Elsewhere, bus service quality *has* improved, and where this has been achieved, it is significantly Volvo whose name frequently appears as vehicle supplier.

When Olympian production came to an end Volvo was ready to introduce a new range of double-deck buses. Among the new low-floor buses exhibited at Coach & Bus '97 was a Volvo double-decker wearing London red paintwork on its Plaxton President bodywork. It was based on a forerunner of what was to become the B7L chassis and featured a longitudinally mounted engine in the corner of the chassis behind the rear axle — an arrangement which reminded many observers of Bristol's VRL, launched at an Earl's Court show more

than 30 years earlier; except that, unlike the Bristol model, the Volvo had its engine placed on the British nearside, excluding any possibility of placing a passenger entrance in this position. The design was not greeted enthusiastically by operators and whilst the B7L went on to form the basis of single-deck chassis (including articulated versions), among the few double-deck applications were those for open-top tour buses, introduced in the UK by the Original London Sightseeing Tour and across Europe by City Sightseeing. A batch of tri-axle double-deck B7Ls with covered top decks was also purchased by First Glasgow.

Meanwhile the Olympian had been largely succeeded by a further new Volvo, the B7TL, a low-floor double-deck chassis with shorter rear overhang, its engine being located transversely across the rear, in a position similar to that pioneered by the Leyland Atlantean 50 years earlier! However, for Far Eastern markets a three-axle low-floor model was introduced with the designation B10TL, the first examples of which were built at Irvine. This was given the model name 'Super Olympian', reflecting just how important the name had become when competing for orders in Asia!

Publicity material for Volvo's Super Olympian three-axle chassis.

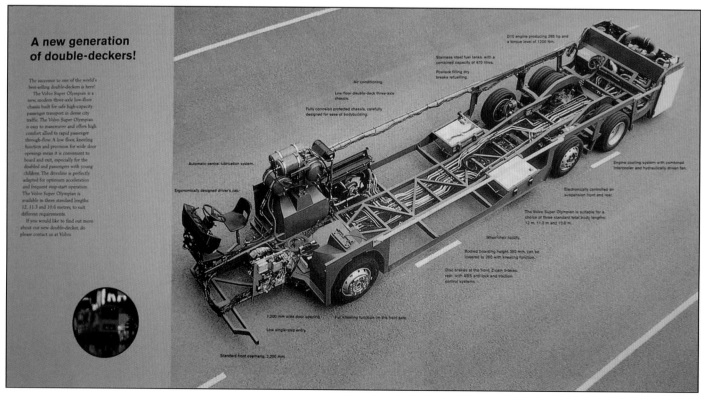

It was largely based on the forward section of a B10L low-floor, single-deck chassis with its rear section perpetuating the Olympian arrangement. After closure of the Irvine factory production of this model was transferred to Poland, while B7TL production went to Sweden. Volvo's bus range continued to do well, but in 2006 these models were superseded for double-deck work by Volvo's B9TL chassis.

With an anticipated operating life of up to 20 years, many Olympians remain in service across all sectors, but the requirement to eliminate step-entrance buses on regular services by 2017 means they may not continue to survive in significant numbers for much longer. Nevertheless, there continues to be a ready market for all second-hand models, and a number have been converted to open-top for tour work — a role that often extends vehicle life.

In Hong Kong, Olympians continue to be extremely prominent with KMB, Citybus and a new company, New World First Bus. This last operator took control of China Motor Bus services with effect from 1 September 1998 and, as its name implies, initially included involvement from

irstGroup. Former CMB Olympians played n important part in establishing NWFB ervices on Hong Kong Island, wearing heir new colours of green, white and range.

Withdrawals of older Hong Kong Olympians have, of course, begun, and a urprising number of three-axle versions have returned to the UK, where they have ntered service with a variety of operators, ncluding within the First and Stagecoach roups.

Finally, a growing number of Olympians are entering preservation, including prototype B45-02 and other significant examples; no doubt numbers will increase over the coming years. The Olympian has been described as the last classic British double-decker, although this definition may be open to debate. However, there is no question that it was an extremely successful design, built in huge numbers, which continues to serve millions of passengers around the world.

Left: **Roe-bodied ON945 became Bristol Omnibus 9554 (A954 SAE) — the last of more than 4,000 Bristol-built buses for Bristol's own operational fleet — and is now preserved. Alongside, restored to its original condition as Devon General 1814 (A686 KDV), is ECW-bodied ON995, the final chassis to be built by Bristol; in its windscreen can be seen displayed the same commemorative board that it carried as a chassis when newly completed. Both vehicles are licensed as Bristols.** *M. S. Curtis*

Left: **Leyland scroll badge as affixed to the engine cover of an Olympian, in this case the final Bristol-built example.**

Far left: **Bristol and B45 badges, as displayed on preserved Bristol 9554.**

Appendices

Leyland Olympian production (including chassis built at Bristol)

Customers (UK / IoM)

NBC

Alder Valley	10
Alder Valley North	3
Bristol / Cheltenham / Gloucester	75
Crosville	107
Cumberland	2
Devon General	7
East Midland / Mansfield	36
East Yorkshire	11
Eastern National	35
Hampshire Bus	5
Lincolnshire	3
London Country / Green Line	90
Maidstone & District	17
Midland Red East / Midland Fox	14
Midland Red North	13
Midland Red South	17
National Welsh	10
Northern	91
(City of) Oxford	24
PMT (Potteries)	15
Red Bus (North Devon)	2
Ribble	80
South Wales	7
Southern Vectis	17
Trent	24
United	68
United Counties	20
Wessex (National Travel West)	1
West Riding / Yorkshire Woollen	111
West Yorkshire / York	63
Western National	8
Wilts & Dorset	5
Yorkshire Traction	73

SBG

Central Scottish	10
Eastern Scottish	55
Fife Scottish	10
Highland Scottish	24
Lowland Scottish	2
Midland Scottish	1
Northern Scottish	88
Strathtay Scottish	9

London Transport / London Buses

London Buses / London Coaches	265
Bexleybus	28
London United	23
Leaside Buses	40

PTE / PTC

Greater Manchester	300
Merseyside / Merseybus	85
South Yorkshire	3
Strathclyde	101
Tyne & Wear / Busways	75
West Yorkshire / Yorkshire Rider	224

Municipal

Blackpool	6
Bournemouth	20
Cardiff	36
Chester	6
Colchester	9
Derby	7
Eastbourne	14
Grampian	30
Grimsby-Cleethorpes	4
Ipswich	1
Lincoln	7
Lothian	296
Maidstone	18
Northampton	6
Nottingham	4
Plymouth	3
Preston	17
Reading	15
Rhymney Valley	3
Rossendale	1
Southampton	9
Southend	5
Warrington	6

Independent

A1 Service, Ardrossan	6
Armchair, Brentford	29
Atlas Bus, Harlesden	9
BTS, Borehamwood	14
R. Bullock, Cheadle	2
Capital Citybus, Dagenham	37
Chambers, Bures	3
Ensignbus, Purfleet	13
Fareway, Liverpool	10
Hedingham	1
Limebourne, London	2
London Buslines, Isleworth	33
Metrobus, Orpington	16
OK, Bishop Auckland	6
Sheffield Omnibus	5
South Notts, Gotham	2
South Yorkshire, Pontefract	8
Stevenson's, Uttoxeter	2

Customers (export)

Total (Leyland Olympian)   5,581

The badges applied to an Athens vehicle, with 'Olympian' written in Greek.

Volvo Olympian production

Customers (UK)

Ex London Buses *(see also 'Stagecoach')*
CentreWest / Orpington Buses	47
London Central	107
London General	85
London United	73
Metroline	38

Ex PTE / PTC *(see also 'First' and 'Stagecoach')*
Merseybus	58
Strathclyde / Greater Glasgow	64
Yorkshire Rider	25

Municipal / ex municipal *
(see also 'Arriva' and 'Stagecoach')
Blackpool	6
*City Rider *(Derby)*	5
Ipswich Buses	3
Lothian	134
Nottingham City Transport	42
Rossendale	2
*Southampton CityBus	6
*Southend Transport	5

Ex NBC *(see also 'Arriva', 'First' and 'Stagecoac[h]')*
Cambus	
City Line / Badgerline *(Bristol)*	3(
East Yorkshire / Scarborough & District	4:
Go Coastline	2:
Kentish Bus	8
London & Country	2(
Maidstone & District	3:
Midland Fox	1:
Northumbria	1:
Road Car *(Lincolnshire)*	8
Selby & District	:
The Shires	1(
Solent Blue Line	(
Southern Vectis	15
Sovereign	8
Tiverton & District *(North Devon)*	:
Western National	4
Yorkshire Coastliner	17

Ex SBG *(see also 'First' and 'Stagecoach')*
Kelvin Central Buses	23
Strathtay	12

Independent *(where not covered above)*
Armchair, Brentford	7
Blue Bus, Horwich	5
R. Bullock, Cheadle	11
Cambridge Coach Services	2
Capital Citybus, Dagenham	46
Chambers, Bures	1
The Delaine, Bourne	6
Finglands, Manchester	9
Harris Bus, West Thurrock	35
Hedingham	1
Liverbus, Liverpool	3
London Suburban Bus	16
Metrobus, Orpington	47

Arriva
Cymru	7
Derby	11
Fox County	27
The Shires	15

First *(standard specification)*
City Line / Badgerline *(Bristol)*	30
Glasgow *(Strathclyde Buses)*	60
Leeds / Bradford / Calderline *(Yorkshire Rider)*	60
Manchester *(Greater Manchester North)*	10
SMT *(Midland Bluebird / Lowland)*	38

Volvo badge and Olympian lettering — the latter applied as a transfer.

Stagecoach *(standard specification)*

.1 Service	21
Bluebird	6
Burnley & Pendle	12
Busways	40
Cambus	30
Coastline Buses *(Sussex Coastline)*	41
Devon *(Bayline / Devon General)*	4
East Kent	36
East London	136
East Midland	32
Grimsby-Cleethorpes	15
Hampshire Bus / Hants & Surrey *(Stagecoach South)*	39
Kingston-upon-Hull	6
Manchester *(Greater Manchester South)*	67
Midland Red *(Midland Red South)*	7
Oxford *(Thames Transit)*	26
Red & White	6
Ribble	35
Selkent	94
South Coast Buses	15
Transit *(Cleveland Transit)*	15
United Counties	51
Viscount	36

Demonstrators etc
Volvo Bus UK *(demonstrators / test chassis)* 5

Customers (export)

Ireland
Dublin Bus	465
Kenneally, Waterford	2
Dualway, Rathcoole	2
Morton, Dublin	2

Singapore
Singapore Bus Service	571

Hong Kong
China Motor Bus	64
Kowloon Motor Bus	894
Long Win	15
Citybus	454
Stagecoach Hong Kong	6
Kowloon–Canton Railway	15
Hong Kong Air Cargo	2
China Light & Power	2

Total (Volvo Olympian) **4,717**

Chassis

Leyland Olympian

Bristol	1,003*
Leyland / Workington	4,578
Total	5,581

* excludes chassis dismantled and reassembled at Workington

Volvo Olympian

Total	4,717

Bodywork

Leyland Olympian

Alexander	2,665
East Lancs	95
ECW	1,470
Leyland	197
Marshall	20
Northern Counties	788
Optare	42
Roe	299
not bodied	5
Total	5,581

Volvo Olympian

Alexander	3,459
East Lancs	164
Northern Counties	1,091
not bodied	3
Total	4,717

Bibliography

Books

Gavin Booth: *Rear-Engined Double-Deckers*
(Ian Allan, 1987)

Stewart J. Brown: *Buses Annual 1991*
(Ian Allan, 1990)

M. G. Doggett and A. A. Townsin: *ECW
1965-87* (Venture Publications, 1994)

Doug Jack: *Beyond Reality:
Leyland Bus – the twilight years*
(Venture Publications, 1994)

Mike Davies: *Hong Kong Buses Vol III:
Citybus Limited* (DTS 1995)

Doug Jack: *The Volvo Bus*
(Venture Publications, 1997)

A. A. Townsin: *The Bristol Story Part II:
1952-83* (Venture Publications, 2000)

Doug Jack: *The Volvo Truck and Bus
Irvine Factory* (Condie, 2000)

Malcolm R. White: *Coachwork by
Eastern Coach Works* (Coastal, 2007)

Danny C. Y. Chan: 'Hong Kong Bus Handbooks'
(Northcord Transport)

Stanley Yung: *The Fleet Directory of
Hong Kong Buses* (BSi/DTS, 2003/4)

various Omnibus Society and PSV Circle
publications

Magazines

Bristol Passenger (Bristol Interest Circle,
1978 to date)

Buses and Buses Illustrated (Ian Allan, 1949
to date)

Buses Focus No 16 (Ian Allan, 2000)

Motor Transport / Bus & Coach
(ibpa/Transport Press, 1970-86)

London Bus Magazine (LOTS Spring 2003,
Autumn 2004)

Other books by the same author

Bristol — A Century on the Road
(Glasney Press, 1978)

Bristol Buses in Camera (Ian Allan, 1984)

Bus Monographs 5: Bristol RE
(Ian Allan, 1987)

Bristol VR (Ian Allan, 1994)

Bristol Omnibus Services — The Green Years
jointly with Mike Walker
(Millstream Books, 2007)

Bristol Lodekka (Ian Allan, 2009)

Dominated by Olympians, this intriguing line-up of Southern Vectis vehicles at Newport, Isle of Wight, was recorded in October 1998. Nearest the camera is Bristol-built Leyland/ECW 689 (RDL 689X), while beyond are Leyland/Northern Counties 743, Volvo/Northern Counties 750, Bristol VRT/ECW 683, Leyland Olympian/Northern Counties 739 (with round headlights), Bristol-built Leyland Olympian/ECW 695, Bristol LHS/ECW 203, all-Leyland Olympians 724 and 720 and finally a further all-Leyland vehicle from the same batch. *M. S. Curtis*